THIS BOOK BELONGS TO

START DATE

MONTH   DAY   YEAR

SHE READS TRUTH™

© 2017 She Reads Truth, LLC
All rights reserved.

ISBN 978-1-946282-26-2

All Scripture is taken from the Christian Standard Bible®, Copyright © 2017
by Holman Bible Publishers. Used by permission. Christian Standard Bible®
and CSB® are federally registered trademarks of Holman Bible Publishers.

Photography © 2017 Jordan & Landon Thompson, Landon Jacob Photography
(Cover, 4, 9, 10, 26, 35, 44, 49, 58, 69, 92, 116). Used by permission.

SEEK GOD AND LIVE:

THE PROPHECIES OF JOEL, AMOS, OBADIAH, JONAH, AND MICAH

SHE READS TRUTH

Nashville, Tennessee

Sins cannot be undone,
only forgiven.

—IGOR STRAVINKSY

Have you ever done something that was honestly deplorable, something you felt desperate to take back as soon as it was done? Even the memory of it can grind you down and make your fingers ache with regret. Shakespeare calls this "an expense of spirit in a waste of shame."

The Minor Prophets show us this same devastating effect of sin.

There isn't much that is minor about these books of the Bible. We call them "minor" because they contain fewer words than the Major Prophets, like Isaiah and Jeremiah, but their words carry just as much weight. It's sobering to read about plagues, wrath, and judgment. Between the locusts and hunger and fire prophesied in these books, it is evident that sin is utterly devastating.

The Old Testament prophets speak with the authority of God's Son, calling out sin and speaking holy judgment. By their words we witness the necessary judgment for sin, the very judgment that Christ took for us.

We can't take our sin back. We can't unsay and undo the shameful things we've done. But the Minor Prophets give us real hope. **The judgment for our sins is massive, but that is precisely the judgment that Jesus paid on our behalf.**

This book presents five Minor Prophets in one cohesive study: Joel, Amos, Obadiah, Jonah, and Micah. Along with the full text of each book, you'll find a timeline to help you place their prophecies in historical and biblical context, guides for reading and understanding biblical prophecy, and a helpful introduction to each of these five short books. Our prayer is that these resources not only equip you to better read and understand God's Word, but also point you to Christ's deep love for us.

I am incredibly thankful to be a part of this community of women. We aren't at all perfect, but we are committed to reading Scripture together—a simple goal that can be difficult to execute. I am grateful to stand with you in this daily walk of faith.

May God meet you as you read the prophecies of Joel, Amos, Obadiah, Jonah, and Micah.

Rebecca

Rebecca Faires
EDITOR

HOW TO USE THIS BOOK

She Reads Truth is a community of women dedicated to reading the Word of God every day. The Bible is living and active, breathed out by God, and we confidently hold it higher than anything we can do or say. This book focuses primarily on Scripture with helpful elements throughout.

We've included study notes in the sidebar on how to read these prophets and their prophecies.

The pinwheel indicates which week and book you are in as you move through the study.

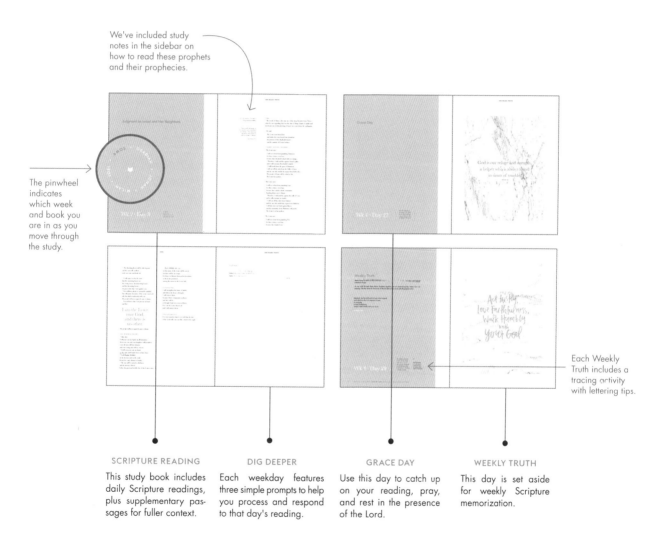

SCRIPTURE READING

This study book includes daily Scripture readings, plus supplementary passages for fuller context.

DIG DEEPER

Each weekday features three simple prompts to help you process and respond to that day's reading.

GRACE DAY

Use this day to catch up on your reading, pray, and rest in the presence of the Lord.

WEEKLY TRUTH

This day is set aside for weekly Scripture memorization.

Each Weekly Truth includes a tracing activity with lettering tips.

Introductions to these Minor Prophets are located at the start of each book. Learn the history and significance of each one as you read.

Design on Purpose

As our design team prepared to create a study book that covered five Minor Prophets, we recognized the need for a quiet, subdued reverence toward the prophetic text. We didn't want design to get in the way of, or feel incongruous with, the subject matter. Instead, we created a mood board that would complement the tone of the content with soft creams and warm blush tones.

We began with inspiration found in a modern travel magazine featuring tilework, ivory, and a warm rose flood of color on the pages. This would be our color palette.

From there, we decided to scatter photography throughout the book, featuring images from Landon Jacob Photography, whom we'd also used for our *Ruth: Fields of Provision* book. This time we focused on the theme of vision, using scenes of nature, color, and light. The image of warm hanging lights on the cover was an exciting find, and immediately made us think of the way the Old Testament prophets were, in their own way, a light in the darkness, revealing who God was and what was to come.

The interior layout was inspired by courtroom documents and collegiate newspapers, giving a nod to the classic "lawsuit" format of many Old Testament prophecies. We left-aligned the text for ease of reading and scanning, setting all Scripture in a traditional serif typeface.

You're likely to see Carrara marble just about anywhere you look these days (in foodie magazines, furniture stores, and coffee shops galore), but we incorporated this marble texture for more than just its ubiquity. The strong stone texture represents the difficult but just prophecies you'll read about in Joel, Amos, Obadiah, Jonah, and Micah.

Finally, one of our favorite details was added to each Weekly Truth spread in this book. As you memorize the key verses, we've created an opportunity for you to hand-letter over the artwork yourself. Use markers, pens, paint brushes, or colored pencils—whatever you have handy—to trace over the faint artwork while you meditate on the Truth it contains. And in case you love how it turns out, we've removed the page numbers and heading from these pages so you can tear it out and put it on display!

We hope you love the way this book came together as much as we do. God's Word does not need anything from us. There is nothing we can do to make it more important and relevant than it already is. In the She Reads Truth creative department, we simply hope to present Scripture in a way that is accessible and aesthetically beautiful, and we hope we've accomplished that for you here. Enjoy!

Table of Contents

Long ago God spoke to the fathers by the prophets at different times and in different ways. In these last days, he has spoken to us by his Son. God has appointed him heir of all things and made the universe through him. Hebrews 1:1-2

How to Read Prophets and Prophecy

Much of the Old Testament is made up of books of prophecy. To understand them, it is helpful to know how these prophets and their messages originally functioned among God's people.

OLD TESTAMENT

Prophets

They were appointed by God.

Prophets did not appoint themselves. The Lord pronounced harsh judgment on false prophets because they assumed authority but did not speak God's Word.

JEREMIAH 14:14-16, JONAH 1:1-2

They were messengers.

Prophets in the Old Testament were people called to deliver a message from God. Their words were not their own.

AMOS 7:14-15, MICAH 1:1

They were insiders.

Prophets usually belonged to the people God called them to address. Their message applied to themselves as well as to their audience.

ISAIAH 6:1-10, AMOS 1:1

They had authority.

Prophets held their office in the same way priests and kings did. They were given the authority to speak God's truth to people in power without fear of retribution.

2 SAMUEL 11:27-12:14, MICAH 3:1

OLD TESTAMENT

Prophecy

It was seldom a new message.

Most of the prophets did not deliver new laws. They usually called Israel to obey God's existing law.
JEREMIAH 2:8-9, OBADIAH 1:15-18

It was read aloud.

Prophecies were originally delivered as messages spoken in public. The prophets were heard before they were read.
DEUTERONOMY 18:18, AMOS 3:1

It was all relational.

Although the prophetic books often deal with concepts like famine, displacement, and God's judgment, the fact that they exist shows that God is in an ongoing relationship with His audience.
JOEL 2:12-14, MICAH 6:3-5

The darker it gets, the bigger the cross appears.

The truth of brokenness and sin is hopeless apart from a redeemer. The Old Testament prophets show this with bleak imagery. Christ went to the cross to atone for the darkest realities described in the prophetic books.
AMOS 1:13-15, 1 PETER 2:6-10

RETURN TO THE LORD YOUR GOD

01 Introduction

Joel

Tear your hearts,
not just your clothes,
and return to the
LORD your God.
For he is gracious
and compassionate,
slow to anger,
abounding in
faithful love,
and he relents from
sending disaster.

—JOEL 2:13

On the Timeline:

While the book of Joel is difficult to date, many scholars believe it was written around 830 B.C. Joel's message was given to the nation of Judah, the southern kingdom in Israel, during the height of the monarchy. According to this date, Joel's message would have been given to Judah roughly 250 years before the Babylonian exile (586 B.C.).

A Little Background:

The book of Joel is one of the shortest in the Old Testament. Its author, Joel, is the son of Pethuel. He is not easily identified with the other Joels of Scripture (1 Samuel 8:2; 1 Chronicles 4:35; Ezra 10:43; Nehemiah 11:9), leaving us only this book to know him, his calling from God, and his message. The book itself gives no biographical information other than his father's name.

Message & Purpose:

Joel's message was concerned primarily with motivating repentance by proclaiming the Day of the Lord. The locust plague is understood as judgment from God and a harbinger of the Day of the Lord (1:2-20, especially v. 15). Joel also announced an even worse judgment—one that would come through a human army (2:1-11).

The phrase "Day of the LORD" is prominent in the book of Joel and describes the judgment day of God. That judgment could be directed both against the nation of Judah and against the "nations" as a whole. In addition to the more general theme of judgment, Joel also pointed to a day when God will make Himself known through His judgments.

SOME DISTINCTIVES:

- The name Joel means "The LORD is God."

- Joel focuses on "The Day of the LORD," which he mentions five times (Joel 1:15, 2:1, 2:11, 2:31, 3:15).

- Joel is written almost exclusively in poetic verse.

- Joel's message comes during a devastating locust plague (1:2-16).

- Joel gives a call to repent and the promise of mercy (1:13-20, 2:12-14).

- Joel promises that the Lord is with His people and will keep His covenant (2:18-27, 3:17).

- Joel foretells the coming Holy Spirit (2:28-32).

Joel's Prophecy

Wk 1 · Day 1

JOEL 1:1-14
ISAIAH 17:10-11
ACTS 2:17-21

Joel 1:1-14

[1] The word of the LORD that came to Joel son of Pethuel:

A PLAGUE OF LOCUSTS

[2] Hear this, you elders;
listen, all you inhabitants of the land.
Has anything like this ever happened in your days
or in the days of your ancestors?
[3] Tell your children about it,
and let your children tell their children,
and their children the next generation.
[4] What the devouring locust has left,
the swarming locust has eaten;
what the swarming locust has left,
the young locust has eaten;
and what the young locust has left,
the destroying locust has eaten.

[5] Wake up, you drunkards, and weep;
wail, all you wine drinkers,
because of the sweet wine,
for it has been taken from your mouth.
[6] For a nation has invaded my land,
powerful and without number;
its teeth are the teeth of a lion,
and it has the fangs of a lioness.
[7] It has devastated my grapevine
and splintered my fig tree.
It has stripped off its bark and thrown it away;
its branches have turned white.
[8] Grieve like a young woman dressed in sackcloth,
mourning for the husband of her youth.
[9] Grain and drink offerings have been cut off
from the house of the LORD;
the priests, who are ministers of the LORD, mourn.
[10] The fields are destroyed;
the land grieves;
indeed, the grain is destroyed;
the new wine is dried up;
and the fresh oil fails.

¹¹ Be ashamed, you farmers,

wail, you vinedressers,

over the wheat and the barley,

because the harvest of the field has perished.

¹² The grapevine is dried up,

and the fig tree is withered;

the pomegranate, the date palm, and the apple—

all the trees of the orchard—have withered.

Indeed, human joy has dried up.

¹³ Dress in sackcloth and lament, you priests;

wail, you ministers of the altar.

Come and spend the night in sackcloth,

you ministers of my God,

because grain and drink offerings

are withheld from the house of your God.

¹⁴ Announce a sacred fast;

proclaim an assembly!

Gather the elders

and all the residents of the land

at the house of the LORD your God,

and cry out to the LORD.

Isaiah 17:10-11

¹⁰ For you have forgotten the God of your salvation,

and you have failed to remember

the rock of your strength;

therefore you will plant beautiful plants

and set out cuttings from exotic vines.

¹¹ On the day that you plant,

you will help them to grow,

and in the morning

you will help your seed to sprout,

but the harvest will vanish

on the day of disease and incurable pain.

Acts 2:17-21

¹⁷ And it will be in the last days, says God,

that I will pour out my Spirit on all people;

then your sons and your daughters will prophesy,

your young men will see visions,

and your old men will dream dreams.

¹⁸ I will even pour out my Spirit

on my servants in those days, both men and women

and they will prophesy.

¹⁹ I will display wonders in the heaven above

and signs on the earth below:

blood and fire and a cloud of smoke.

²⁰ The sun will be turned to darkness

and the moon to blood

before the great and glorious day of the Lord comes.

²¹ Then everyone who calls

on the name of the Lord will be saved.

Dig Deeper

Observe. What is happening in the text?

Reflect. What does it teach me about God?

Apply. What is my response?

DATE

The Day of the Lord

Wk 1 · Day 2

JOEL 1:15-20
JOEL 2:1-11
PSALM 43:4
ROMANS 10:13

Joel 1:15-20
THE DAY OF THE LORD

¹⁵ Woe because of that day!

For the day of the LORD is near

and will come as devastation from the Almighty.
¹⁶ Hasn't the food been cut off
before our eyes,
joy and gladness
from the house of our God?
¹⁷ The seeds lie shriveled in their casings.
The storehouses are in ruin,
and the granaries are broken down,
because the grain has withered away.
¹⁸ How the animals groan!
The herds of cattle wander in confusion
since they have no pasture.
Even the flocks of sheep and goats suffer punishment.
¹⁹ I call to you, LORD,
for fire has consumed
the pastures of the wilderness,
and flames have devoured
all the trees of the orchard.
²⁰ Even the wild animals cry out to you,
for the river beds are dried up,
and fire has consumed
the pastures of the wilderness.

Joel 2:1-11

¹ Blow the horn in Zion;
sound the alarm on my holy mountain!
Let all the residents of the land tremble,
for the day of the LORD is coming;
in fact, it is near—
² a day of darkness and gloom,
a day of clouds and total darkness,
like the dawn spreading over the mountains;

a great and strong people appears,
such as never existed in ages past
and never will again
in all the generations to come.

³ A fire devours in front of them,
and behind them a flame blazes.
The land in front of them
is like the garden of Eden,
but behind them,
it is like a desert wasteland;
there is no escape from them.
⁴ Their appearance is like that of horses,
and they gallop like war horses.
⁵ They bound on the tops of the mountains.
Their sound is like the sound of chariots,
like the sound of fiery flames consuming stubble,
like a mighty army deployed for war.

⁶ Nations writhe in horror before them;
all faces turn pale.
⁷ They attack as warriors attack;
they scale walls as men of war do.
Each goes on his own path,
and they do not change their course.
⁸ They do not push each other;
each proceeds on his own path.
They dodge the arrows, never stopping.
⁹ They storm the city;
they run on the wall;
they climb into the houses;
they enter through the windows like thieves.

¹⁰ The earth quakes before them;
the sky shakes.

The sun and moon grow dark, and the stars cease their shining.

¹¹ The Lord makes his voice heard
in the presence of his army.
His camp is very large;
those who carry out his command are powerful.
Indeed, the day of the Lord is terrible and dreadful—
who can endure it?

Psalm 43:4
Then I will come to the altar of God,
to God, my greatest joy.
I will praise you with the lyre,
God, my God.

Romans 10:13
For everyone who calls on the name of the Lord
will be saved.

Dig Deeper

Observe. What is happening in the text?

Reflect. What does it teach me about God?

Apply. What is my response?

DATE

God's Call for Repentance

JOEL · AMOS · OBADIAH · JONAH · MICAH

Wk 1 · Day 3

JOEL 2:12-17
ZEPHANIAH 1:7
ROMANS 5:18-21

OLD TESTAMENT PROPHECY
It was all relational.

Although the prophetic books often deal with concepts like famine, displacement, and God's judgment, the fact that they exist shows that God is in an ongoing relationship with His audience.

See Joel 2:12-14

Joel 2:12-17
GOD'S CALL FOR REPENTANCE

12 Even now—
   this is the LORD's declaration—
turn to me with all your heart,
with fasting, weeping, and mourning.
13 Tear your hearts,
not just your clothes,
and return to the LORD your God.
For he is gracious and compassionate,
slow to anger, abounding in faithful love,
and he relents from sending disaster.
14 Who knows? He may turn and relent
and leave a blessing behind him,
so you can offer grain and wine
to the LORD your God.

15 Blow the horn in Zion!
Announce a sacred fast;
proclaim an assembly.
16 Gather the people;
sanctify the congregation;
assemble the aged;
gather the infants,
even babies nursing at the breast.
Let the groom leave his bedroom,
and the bride her honeymoon chamber.
17 Let the priests, the LORD's ministers,
weep between the portico and the altar.
Let them say:
"Have pity on your people, LORD,
and do not make your inheritance a disgrace,
an object of scorn among the nations.
Why should it be said among the peoples,
'Where is their God?'"

Zephaniah 1:7
Be silent in the presence of the Lord GOD,
for the day of the LORD is near.
Indeed, the LORD has prepared a sacrifice;
he has consecrated his guests.

Romans 5:18-21

[18] So then, as through one trespass there is condemnation for everyone, so also through one righteous act there is justification leading to life for everyone. [19] For just as through one man's disobedience the many were made sinners, so also through the one man's obedience the many will be made righteous. [20] The law came along to multiply the trespass. But where sin multiplied, grace multiplied even more [21] so that, just as sin reigned in death, so also grace will reign through righteousness, resulting in eternal life through Jesus Christ our Lord.

Dig Deeper

Observe. What is happening in the text?

Reflect. What does it teach me about God?

Apply. What is my response?

DATE

God's Promise of His Spirit

JOEL 2:18-32
ZECHARIAH 10:6
1 THESSALONIANS 5:2

Joel 2:18-32
GOD'S RESPONSE TO HIS PEOPLE

[18] Then the LORD became jealous for his land and spared his people.
[19] The LORD answered his people:

Look, I am about to send you
grain, new wine, and fresh oil.
You will be satiated with them,
and I will no longer make you
a disgrace among the nations.

[20] I will drive the northerner far from you
and banish him to a dry and desolate land,
his front ranks into the Dead Sea,
and his rear guard into the Mediterranean Sea.
His stench will rise;
yes, his rotten smell will rise,
for he has done astonishing things.

[21] Don't be afraid, land;
rejoice and be glad,
for the LORD has done astonishing things.
[22] Don't be afraid, wild animals,
for the wilderness pastures have turned green,
the trees bear their fruit,
and the fig tree and grapevine yield their riches.
[23] Children of Zion, rejoice and be glad
in the LORD your God,
because he gives you the autumn rain
for your vindication.

He sends showers
for you,
both autumn and
spring rain as before.

²⁴ The threshing floors will be full of grain,
and the vats will overflow
with new wine and fresh oil.

²⁵ I will repay you for the years
that the swarming locust ate,
the young locust, the destroying locust,
and the devouring locust—
my great army that I sent against you.
²⁶ You will have plenty to eat and be satisfied.
You will praise the name of the LORD your God,
who has dealt wondrously with you.
My people will never again be put to shame.
²⁷ You will know that I am present in Israel
and that

I am the LORD your God, and there is no other.

My people will never again be put to shame.

GOD'S PROMISE OF HIS SPIRIT

²⁸ After this
I will pour out my Spirit on all humanity;
then your sons and your daughters will prophesy,
your old men will have dreams,
and your young men will see visions.
²⁹ I will even pour out my Spirit
on the male and female slaves in those days.
³⁰ I will display wonders
in the heavens and on the earth:
blood, fire, and columns of smoke.
³¹ The sun will be turned to darkness
and the moon to blood
before the great and terrible day of the LORD comes.

³² Then everyone who calls
on the name of the LORD will be saved,
for there will be an escape
for those on Mount Zion and in Jerusalem,
as the LORD promised,
among the survivors the LORD calls.

Zechariah 10:6
I will strengthen the house of Judah
and deliver the house of Joseph.
I will restore them
because I have compassion on them,
and they will be
as though I had never rejected them.
For I am the LORD their God,
and I will answer them.

1 Thessalonians 5:2
For you yourselves know very well that the day
of the Lord will come just like a thief in the night.

Dig Deeper

Observe. What is happening in the text?

Reflect. What does it teach me about God?

Apply. What is my response?

DATE

Israel Blessed

Wk 1 · Day 5

JOEL 3
ISAIAH 33:20-22
JEREMIAH 33:1-11

Joel 3
JUDGMENT OF THE NATIONS

¹ Yes, in those days and at that time,
when I restore the fortunes of Judah and Jerusalem,
² I will gather all the nations
and take them to the Valley of Jehoshaphat.
I will enter into judgment with them there
because of my people, my inheritance Israel.
The nations have scattered the Israelites
in foreign countries
and divided up my land.
³ They cast lots for my people;
they bartered a boy for a prostitute
and sold a girl for wine to drink.

⁴ And also: Tyre, Sidon, and all the territories of Philistia—what are you to me? Are you paying me back or trying to get even with me? I will quickly bring retribution on your heads. ⁵ For you took my silver and gold and carried my finest treasures to your temples. ⁶ You sold the people of Judah and Jerusalem to the Greeks to remove them far from their own territory. ⁷ Look, I am about to rouse them up from the place where you sold them; I will bring retribution on your heads. ⁸ I will sell your sons and daughters to the people of Judah, and they will sell them to the Sabeans, to a distant nation, for the LORD has spoken.

⁹ Proclaim this among the nations:
Prepare for holy war;
rouse the warriors;
let all the men of war advance and attack!
¹⁰ Beat your plows into swords
and your pruning knives into spears.
Let even the weakling say, "I am a warrior."
¹¹ Come quickly, all you surrounding nations;
gather yourselves.
Bring down your warriors there, LORD.

¹² Let the nations be roused
and come to the Valley of Jehoshaphat,
for there I will sit down
to judge all the surrounding nations.

¹³ Swing the sickle
because the harvest is ripe.
Come and trample the grapes
because the winepress is full;
the wine vats overflow
because the wickedness of the nations is extreme.

¹⁴ Multitudes, multitudes
in the valley of decision!
For the day of the Lord is near
in the valley of decision.
¹⁵ The sun and moon will grow dark,
and the stars will cease their shining.
¹⁶ The Lord will roar from Zion
and make his voice heard from Jerusalem;
heaven and earth will shake.

> But the Lord
> will be a refuge
> for his people,
> a stronghold for
> the Israelites.

ISRAEL BLESSED

¹⁷ Then you will know
that I am the Lord your God,
who dwells in Zion, my holy mountain.
Jerusalem will be holy,
and foreigners will never overrun it again.
¹⁸ In that day
the mountains will drip with sweet wine,
and the hills will flow with milk.
All the streams of Judah will flow with water,
and a spring will issue from the Lord's house,
watering the Valley of Acacias.
¹⁹ Egypt will become desolate,
and Edom a desert wasteland,
because of the violence done to the people of Judah
in whose land they shed innocent blood.
²⁰ But Judah will be inhabited forever,
and Jerusalem from generation to generation.
²¹ I will pardon their bloodguilt,
which I have not pardoned,
for the Lord dwells in Zion.

Isaiah 33:20-22

²⁰ Look at Zion, the city of our festival times.
Your eyes will see Jerusalem,
a peaceful pasture, a tent that does not wander;
its tent pegs will not be pulled up
nor will any of its cords be loosened.
²¹ For the majestic one, our Lord, will be there,
a place of rivers and broad streams
where ships that are rowed will not go,
and majestic vessels will not pass.
²² For the Lord is our Judge,
the Lord is our Lawgiver,
the Lord is our King.
He will save us.

Jeremiah 33:1-11

ISRAEL'S RESTORATION

¹ While he was still confined in the guard's courtyard, the word of the Lord came to Jeremiah a second time: ² "The Lord who made the earth, the Lord who forms it to establish it, the Lord is his name, says this: ³ Call to me and I will answer you and tell you great and incomprehensible things you do not know. ⁴ For this is what the Lord, the God of Israel, says concerning the houses of this city and the palaces of Judah's kings, the ones torn down for defense against the assault ramps and the sword: ⁵ The people coming to fight the Chaldeans will fill the houses with the corpses of their own men that I strike down in my wrath and rage. I have hidden my face from this city because of all their evil. ⁶ Yet I will certainly bring health and healing to it and will indeed heal them. I will let them experience the abundance of true peace. ⁷ I will restore the fortunes of Judah and of Israel and will rebuild them as in former times. ⁸ I will purify them from all the iniquity they have committed against me, and I will forgive all the iniquities they have committed against me, rebelling against me. ⁹ This city will bear on my behalf a name of joy, praise, and glory before all the nations of the earth, who will hear of all the prosperity I will give them. They will tremble with awe because of all the good and all the peace I will bring about for them.

¹⁰ "This is what the Lord says: In this place, which you say is a ruin, without people or animals—that is, in Judah's cities and Jerusalem's streets that are a desolation without people, without inhabitants, and without animals—there will be heard again ¹¹ a sound of joy and gladness, the voice of the groom and the bride, and the voice of those saying,

Give thanks to the Lord of Armies,
for the Lord is good;
his faithful love endures forever

as they bring thank offerings to the temple of the Lord. For I will restore the fortunes of the land as in former times, says the Lord."

Dig Deeper

Observe. What is happening in the text?

Reflect. What does it teach me about God?

Apply. What is my response?

DATE

A GOD OF MERCY

Give Thanks for the Book of Joel

The book of Joel is good news because it shows the Creator and Redeemer God of all the universe in complete control of His creation. Joel reminds us that the God of judgment is also a God of mercy, who stands ready to redeem and restore when His people come before Him in repentance. This book points to a time when the Spirit of God would be present upon all people—a prophecy fulfilled on the day of Pentecost (Acts 2:17-21).

Grace Day

Wk 1 · Day 6

Take this day as an
opportunity to catch
up on your reading,
pray, and rest in the
presence of the Lord.

But where sin multiplied, grace
multiplied even more so that,
just as sin reigned in death,
so also grace will reign through
righteousness, resulting in
eternal life through Jesus
Christ our Lord.

— ROMANS 5:20-21

Weekly Truth

Memorizing Scripture is one of the best ways to carry God-breathed truth, instruction, and reproof wherever we go.

As we walk through these Minor Prophets together, we will memorize key verses from our reading. The key verse for the book of Joel calls us to true repentance.

Tear your hearts,
not just your clothes,
and return to the LORD your God.
For he is gracious and compassionate,
slow to anger, abounding in faithful love,
and he relents from sending disaster.

—JOEL 2:13

We left the artwork on the facing page extra light, so you can enjoy a lesson in hand-lettering while meditating on the key verse for Joel.

↓

Our favorite way to letter in this style is using a colored Sharpie® pen.

Wk 1 · Day 7

FIND THE CORRESPONDING **MEMORY CARD** PERFORATED IN THE BACK OF YOUR BOOK.

RETURN TO THE LORD YOUR GOD

But let
JUSTICE
flow like water
& RIGHTEOUSNESS,
like an unfailing
Stream

02 Introduction

Amos

But let justice flow like water, and righteousness, like an unfailing stream.

—AMOS 5:24

On the Timeline:

Amos prophesied during the reigns of Uzziah of Judah (792–740 B.C.) and Jeroboam II of Israel (793–753 B.C.). This was a time of great prosperity for both nations, and the weakened condition of their enemies meant great military success. Amos's prophecy to Israel occurred around 760 B.C., about 40 years before Israel was destroyed by Assyria and 175 years before Judah's destruction and exile.

A Little Background:

Amos was a shepherd from Tekoa, a village about 10 miles south of Jerusalem. God called Amos to go north and prophesy against Samaria and the kingdom of Israel. Though we do not know how long he was in the north, it appears to have been a fairly short time. Amos provoked a great deal of opposition and anger, as illustrated by his encounter with Amaziah, the priest of Bethel (7:10-17). He wrote his book, a summary of his prophecies, after his return to Judah.

Message & Purpose:

God's right to judge the earth was the centerpiece of Amos's message. He proclaimed that God is impartial and fair, judging each nation appropriately, and neither Jew nor Gentile is exempt from divine judgment. In Amos's prophecies, the Gentiles are punished for their crimes against humanity, while the Jews are judged by the demands of the Mosaic law (1:3–2:3; 2:4-5). Even after judgment, when it seems all hope is lost (9:1-4), God is able to bring about redemption and salvation (9:13-15). Israel's hope—and humanity's hope—is in the line of David, which God will raise up to establish His kingdom (9:11-12). We now know this prophecy is fulfilled in Jesus Christ.

SOME DISTINCTIVES:

- The name Amos means "burden bearer."

- Nothing is known about Amos except that he was a shepherd from Tekoa.

- Amos focuses on the justice of God. Judgment awaits God's enemies (Amos 1:2-2:5) as well as His own people (2:6-9:10).

- Amos is written almost exclusively in poetic verse.

- Amos is composed of two groups of judgment oracles: those addressed to Israel's neighbors (1:2-2:16), and those addressed to God's own people (3:1-6:14).

- The last chapters of Amos are comprised of five visions of coming judgment: locusts (7:1-3), fire (7:4-6), a plumb line (7:7-9), a basket of summer fruit (8:1-14), and the Lord beside the altar (9:1-6).

Judgment on Israel and Her Neighbors

Wk 2 · Day 8

AMOS 1
AMOS 2
PSALM 33:13-22
ISAIAH 42:10-13

OLD TESTAMENT PROPHETS
They were insiders.

They usually belonged to the people God called them to address. Their message applied to themselves as well as to their audience.

See Amos 1:1

Amos 1

¹ The words of Amos, who was one of the sheep breeders from Tekoa— what he saw regarding Israel in the days of King Uzziah of Judah and Jeroboam son of Jehoash, king of Israel, two years before the earthquake.

² He said:

The LORD roars from Zion
and makes his voice heard from Jerusalem;
the pastures of the shepherds mourn,
and the summit of Carmel withers.

JUDGMENT ON ISRAEL'S NEIGHBORS

³ The LORD says:

I will not relent from punishing Damascus
for three crimes, even four,
because they threshed Gilead with iron sledges.
⁴ Therefore, I will send fire against Hazael's palace,
and it will consume Ben-hadad's citadels.
⁵ I will break down the gates of Damascus.
I will cut off the ruler from the Valley of Aven,
and the one who wields the scepter from Beth-eden.
The people of Aram will be exiled to Kir.
The LORD has spoken.

⁶ The LORD says:

I will not relent from punishing Gaza
for three crimes, even four,
because they exiled a whole community,
handing them over to Edom.
⁷ Therefore, I will send fire against the walls of Gaza,
and it will consume its citadels.
⁸ I will cut off the ruler from Ashdod,
and the one who wields the scepter from Ashkelon.
I will also turn my hand against Ekron,
and the remainder of the Philistines will perish.
The LORD God has spoken.

⁹ The LORD says:

I will not relent from punishing Tyre
for three crimes, even four,
because they handed over

a whole community of exiles to Edom
and broke a treaty of brotherhood.
¹⁰ Therefore, I will send fire against the walls of Tyre,
and it will consume its citadels.

¹¹ The Lᴏʀᴅ says:

I will not relent from punishing Edom
for three crimes, even four,
because he pursued his brother with the sword.
He stifled his compassion,
his anger tore at him continually,
and he harbored his rage incessantly.
¹² Therefore, I will send fire against Teman,
and it will consume the citadels of Bozrah.

¹³ The Lᴏʀᴅ says:

I will not relent from punishing the Ammonites
for three crimes, even four,
because they ripped open
the pregnant women of Gilead
in order to enlarge their territory.
¹⁴ Therefore, I will set fire to the walls of Rabbah,
and it will consume its citadels.
There will be shouting on the day of battle
and a violent wind on the day of the storm.
¹⁵ Their king and his princes
will go into exile together.
The Lᴏʀᴅ has spoken.

Amos 2

¹ The Lᴏʀᴅ says:

I will not relent from punishing Moab
for three crimes, even four,
because he burned the bones
of the king of Edom to lime.
² Therefore, I will send fire against Moab,
and it will consume the citadels of Kerioth.
Moab will die with a tumult,
with shouting and the sound of the ram's horn.
³ I will cut off the judge from the land
and kill all its officials with him.
The Lᴏʀᴅ has spoken.

OLD TESTAMENT
PROPHECY
The darker
it gets, the
bigger the
cross appears.

The truth of
brokenness and
sin is hopeless
apart from a
redeemer. The
Old Testament
prophets show
this with bleak
imagery. Christ
went to the cross
to atone for the
darkest realities
described in the
prophetic books.

See Amos
1:13-15

JUDGMENT ON JUDAH

⁴ The Lᴏʀᴅ says:

I will not relent from punishing Judah
for three crimes, even four,
because they have rejected the instruction of the Lord
and have not kept his statutes.
The lies that their ancestors followed
have led them astray.
⁵ Therefore, I will send fire against Judah,
and it will consume the citadels of Jerusalem.

JUDGMENT ON ISRAEL

⁶ The Lᴏʀᴅ says:

I will not relent from punishing Israel
for three crimes, even four,
because they sell a righteous person for silver
and a needy person for a pair of sandals.
⁷ They trample the heads of the poor
on the dust of the ground
and obstruct the path of the needy.
A man and his father have sexual relations
with the same girl,
profaning my holy name.
⁸ They stretch out beside every altar
on garments taken as collateral,
and in the house of their God
they drink wine obtained through fines.

⁹ Yet I destroyed the Amorite as Israel advanced;
his height was like the cedars,
and he was as sturdy as the oaks;
I destroyed his fruit above and his roots beneath.
¹⁰ And I brought you from the land of Egypt
and led you forty years in the wilderness
in order to possess the land of the Amorite.
¹¹ I raised up some of your sons as prophets
and some of your young men as Nazirites.
Is this not the case, Israelites?

This is the Lᴏʀᴅ's declaration.

¹² But you made the Nazirites drink wine
and commanded the prophets,
"Do not prophesy."

¹³ Look, I am about to crush you in your place
as a wagon crushes when full of grain.
¹⁴ Escape will fail the swift,
the strong one will not maintain his strength,
and the warrior will not save his life.
¹⁵ The archer will not stand his ground,
the one who is swift of foot
will not save himself,
and the one riding a horse will not save his life.
¹⁶ Even the most courageous of the warriors
will flee naked on that day—
this is the Lord's declaration.

Psalm 33:13-22

¹³ The Lord looks down from heaven;
he observes everyone.
¹⁴ He gazes on all the inhabitants of the earth
from his dwelling place.
¹⁵ He forms the hearts of them all;
he considers all their works.
¹⁶ A king is not saved by a large army;
a warrior will not be rescued by great strength.
¹⁷ The horse is a false hope for safety;
it provides no escape by its great power.

¹⁸ But look, the Lord keeps his eye on those who fear him—
those who depend on his faithful love
¹⁹ to rescue them from death
and to keep them alive in famine.

²⁰ We wait for the Lord;
he is our help and shield.
²¹ For our hearts rejoice in him
because we trust in his holy name.
²² May your faithful love rest on us, Lord,
for we put our hope in you.

Isaiah 42:10-13
A SONG OF PRAISE

¹⁰ Sing a new song to the Lord;
sing his praise from the ends of the earth,
you who go down to the sea with all that fills it,
you coasts and islands with your inhabitants.
¹¹ Let the desert and its cities shout,
the settlements where Kedar dwells cry aloud.
Let the inhabitants of Sela sing for joy;
let them cry out from the mountaintops.
¹² Let them give glory to the Lord
and declare his praise in the coasts and islands.
¹³ The Lord advances like a warrior;
he stirs up his zeal like a soldier.
He shouts, he roars aloud,
he prevails over his enemies.

Dig Deeper

Observe. What is happening in the text?

Reflect. What does it teach me about God?

Apply. What is my response?

DATE

The World of the Minor Prophets

Joel's prophetic ministry

830 BC

850 BC

800 BC

B 835 BC
Joash becomes king of Judah

B 793 BC
Jeroboam II becomes king of Israel

W c. 850 BC
Technique of glazing decorative pottery used in Mesopotamia

W 814 BC
Carthage founded

B 792 BC
Uzziah becomes king of Judah

W c. 800 BC
Earliest surviving sundial used in Egypt

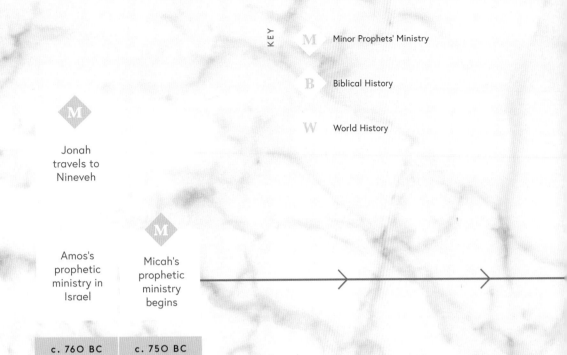

KEY

M Minor Prophets' Ministry

B Biblical History

W World History

M Jonah travels to Nineveh

M Micah's prophetic ministry begins

Amos's prophetic ministry in Israel

c. 760 BC

c. 750 BC

750 BC

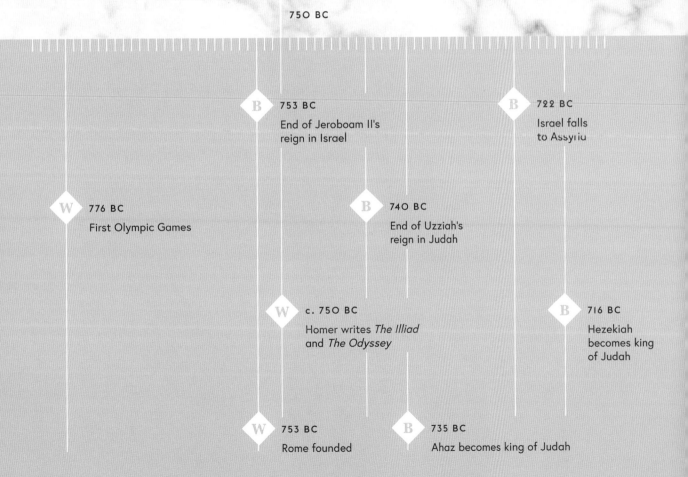

W 776 BC
First Olympic Games

B 753 BC
End of Jeroboam II's reign in Israel

W 753 BC
Rome founded

W c. 750 BC
Homer writes *The Illiad* and *The Odyssey*

B 740 BC
End of Uzziah's reign in Judah

B 735 BC
Ahaz becomes king of Judah

B 722 BC
Israel falls to Assyria

B 716 BC
Hezekiah becomes king of Judah

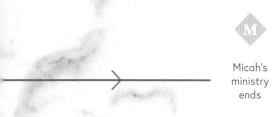

Micah's
ministry
ends

c. 690 BC

700 BC   650 BC

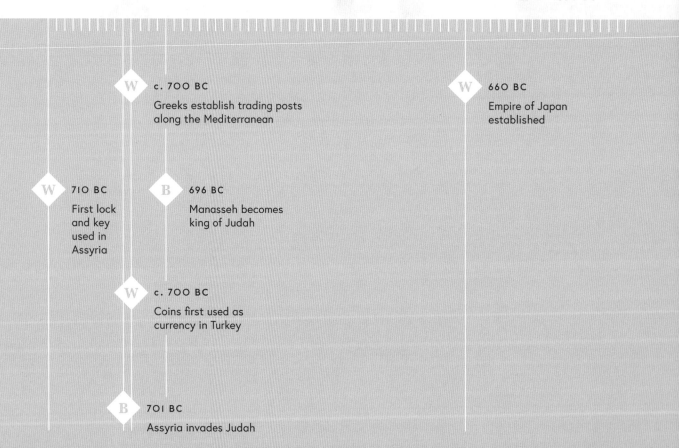

W c. 700 BC

Greeks establish trading posts
along the Mediterranean

W 660 BC

Empire of Japan
established

W 710 BC

First lock
and key
used in
Assyria

B 696 BC

Manasseh becomes
king of Judah

W c. 700 BC

Coins first used as
currency in Turkey

B 701 BC

Assyria invades Judah

Obadiah
prophesies
the
destruction
of Judah

586 BC

600 BC

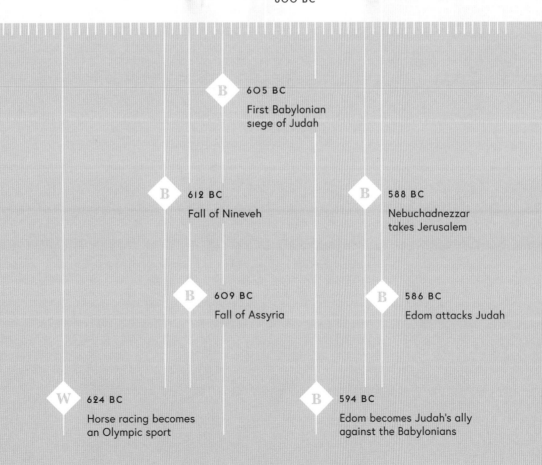

B 605 BC

First Babylonian
siege of Judah

B 612 BC

Fall of Nineveh

B 588 BC

Nebuchadnezzar
takes Jerusalem

B 609 BC

Fall of Assyria

B 586 BC

Edom attacks Judah

W 624 BC

Horse racing becomes
an Olympic sport

B 594 BC

Edom becomes Judah's ally
against the Babylonians

God's Discipline

Wk 2 · Day 9

AMOS 3
AMOS 4
PSALM 65:5-8
ROMANS 11:1-6

OLD TESTAMENT PROPHECY
It was read aloud.

Prophecies were originally
delivered as messages
spoken in public. The
prophets were heard
before they were read.

See Amos 3:1

Amos 3

GOD'S REASONS FOR PUNISHING ISRAEL

¹ Listen to this message that the LORD has spoken against you, Israelites, against the entire clan that I brought from the land of Egypt:

² I have known only you
out of all the clans of the earth;
therefore, I will punish you for all your iniquities.
³ Can two walk together
without agreeing to meet?
⁴ Does a lion roar in the forest
when it has no prey?
Does a young lion growl from its lair
unless it has captured something?
⁵ Does a bird land in a trap on the ground
if there is no bait for it?
Does a trap spring from the ground
when it has caught nothing?
⁶ If a ram's horn is blown in a city,
aren't people afraid?
If a disaster occurs in a city,
hasn't the LORD done it?
⁷ Indeed, the Lord GOD does nothing
without revealing his counsel
to his servants the prophets.
⁸ A lion has roared;
who will not fear?
The Lord GOD has spoken;
who will not prophesy?

⁹ Proclaim on the citadels in Ashdod
and on the citadels in the land of Egypt:
Assemble on the mountains of Samaria,
and see the great turmoil in the city
and the acts of oppression within it.
¹⁰ The people are incapable of doing right—
this is the LORD's declaration—
those who store up violence and destruction
in their citadels.

¹¹ Therefore, the Lord GOD says:

An enemy will surround the land;
he will destroy your strongholds
and plunder your citadels.

¹² The LORD says:

As the shepherd snatches two legs
or a piece of an ear
from the lion's mouth,
so the Israelites who live in Samaria
will be rescued
with only the corner of a bed
or the cushion of a couch.

¹³ Listen and testify against the house of Jacob—
this is the declaration of the Lord GOD,
the God of Armies.

¹⁴ I will punish the altars of Bethel
on the day I punish Israel for its crimes;
the horns of the altar will be cut off
and fall to the ground.
¹⁵ I will demolish the winter house
and the summer house;
the houses inlaid with ivory will be destroyed,
and the great houses will come to an end.

This is the LORD's declaration.

Amos 4

SOCIAL AND SPIRITUAL CORRUPTION

¹ Listen to this message, you cows of Bashan
who are on the hill of Samaria,
women who oppress the poor
and crush the needy,
who say to their husbands,
"Bring us something to drink."

² The Lord GOD has sworn by his holiness:

Look, the days are coming
when you will be taken away with hooks,
every last one of you with fishhooks.
³ You will go through breaches in the wall,
each woman straight ahead,
and you will be driven along toward Harmon.
This is the LORD's declaration.

⁴ Come to Bethel and rebel;
rebel even more at Gilgal!
Bring your sacrifices every morning,
your tenths every three days.
⁵ Offer leavened bread as a thank offering,
and loudly proclaim your freewill offerings,
for that is what you Israelites love to do!
This is the LORD's declaration.

GOD'S DISCIPLINE AND ISRAEL'S APOSTASY

⁶ I gave you absolutely nothing to eat
in all your cities,
a shortage of food in all your communities,

yet you did not return to me.

This is the LORD's declaration.

⁷ I also withheld the rain from you
while there were still three months until harvest.
I sent rain on one city
but no rain on another.
One field received rain
while a field with no rain withered.
⁸ Two or three cities staggered
to another city to drink water
but were not satisfied,
yet you did not return to me.
This is the LORD's declaration.

⁹ I struck you with blight and mildew;
the locust devoured
your many gardens and vineyards,
your fig trees and olive trees,
yet you did not return to me.
This is the LORD's declaration.

¹⁰ I sent plagues like those of Egypt;
I killed your young men with the sword,
along with your captured horses.
I caused the stench of your camp
to fill your nostrils,
yet you did not return to me.
This is the LORD's declaration.

¹¹ I overthrew some of you
as I overthrew Sodom and Gomorrah,
and you were like a burning stick
snatched from a fire,
yet you did not return to me—
This is the LORD's declaration.

¹² Therefore, Israel, that is what I will do to you,
and since I will do that to you,
Israel, prepare to meet your God!
¹³ He is here:
the one who forms the mountains,
creates the wind,
and reveals his thoughts to man,
the one who makes the dawn out of darkness
and strides on the heights of the earth.
The LORD, the God of Armies, is his name.

Psalm 65:5-8

5 You answer us in righteousness,
with awe-inspiring works,
God of our salvation,
the hope of all the ends of the earth
and of the distant seas.
6 You establish the mountains by your power;
you are robed with strength.
7 You silence the roar of the seas,
the roar of their waves,
and the tumult of the nations.
8 Those who live far away are awed by your signs;
you make east and west shout for joy.

Romans 11:1-6

ISRAEL'S REJECTION NOT TOTAL

1 I ask, then, has God rejected his people? Absolutely not! For I too am an Israelite, a descendant of Abraham, from the tribe of Benjamin. 2 God has not rejected his people whom he foreknew. Or don't you know what the Scripture says in the passage about Elijah—how he pleads with God against Israel? 3 Lord, they have killed your prophets and torn down your altars. I am the only one left, and they are trying to take my life! 4 But what was God's answer to him? I have left seven thousand for myself who have not bowed down to Baal. 5 In the same way, then, there is also at the present time a remnant chosen by grace. 6 Now if by grace, then it is not by works; otherwise grace ceases to be grace.

Dig Deeper

Observe. What is happening in the text?

Reflect. What does it teach me about God?

Apply. What is my response?

DATE

Seek God and Live

Wk 2 · Day 10

AMOS 5
MICAH 6:8
PHILIPPIANS 4:8-9

NOTES

Amos 5

LAMENTATION FOR ISRAEL

[1] Listen to this message that I am singing for you, a lament, house of Israel:

[2] She has fallen;
Virgin Israel will never rise again.
She lies abandoned on her land
with no one to raise her up.

[3] For the Lord God says:

The city that marches out a thousand strong
will have only a hundred left,
and the one that marches out a hundred strong
will have only ten left in the house of Israel.

SEEK GOD AND LIVE

[4] For the Lord says to the house of Israel:

Seek me and live!
[5] Do not seek Bethel
or go to Gilgal
or journey to Beer-sheba,
for Gilgal will certainly go into exile,
and Bethel will come to nothing.
[6] Seek the Lord and live,
or he will spread like fire
throughout the house of Joseph;
it will consume everything
with no one at Bethel to extinguish it.
[7] Those who turn justice into wormwood
also throw righteousness to the ground.

[8] The one who made the Pleiades and Orion,
who turns darkness into dawn
and darkens day into night,
who summons the water of the sea
and pours it out over the surface of the earth—
the Lord is his name.
[9] He brings destruction on the strong,
and it falls on the fortress.

¹⁰ They hate the one who convicts the guilty
at the city gate,
and they despise the one who speaks with
integrity.
¹¹ Therefore, because you trample on the poor
and exact a grain tax from him,
you will never live in the houses of cut stone
you have built;
you will never drink the wine
from the lush vineyards
you have planted.
¹² For I know your crimes are many
and your sins innumerable.
They oppress the righteous, take a bribe,
and deprive the poor of justice at the city gates.
¹³ Therefore, those who have insight will
keep silent
at such a time,
for the days are evil.

¹⁴ Pursue good and not evil
so that you may live,
and the LORD, the God of Armies,
will be with you
as you have claimed.
¹⁵ Hate evil and love good;
establish justice in the city gate.
Perhaps the LORD, the God of Armies, will
be gracious
to the remnant of Joseph.

¹⁶ Therefore the LORD, the God of Armies, the
LORD, says:

There will be wailing in all the public squares;
they will cry out in anguish in all the streets.
The farmer will be called on to mourn,
and professional mourners to wail.
¹⁷ There will be wailing in all the vineyards,
for I will pass among you.
The LORD has spoken.

THE DAY OF THE LORD

¹⁸ Woe to you who long for the day of the LORD!
What will the day of the LORD be for you?
It will be darkness and not light.
¹⁹ It will be like a man who flees from a lion
only to have a bear confront him.
He goes home and rests his hand against the wall
only to have a snake bite him.
²⁰ Won't the day of the LORD
be darkness rather than light,
even gloom without any brightness in it?
²¹ I hate, I despise, your feasts!
I can't stand the stench
of your solemn assemblies.
²² Even if you offer me
your burnt offerings and grain offerings,
I will not accept them;
I will have no regard
for your fellowship offerings of fattened cattle.
²³ Take away from me the noise of your songs!
I will not listen to the music of your harps.
²⁴ But let justice flow like water,
and righteousness, like an unfailing stream.

²⁵ "House of Israel, was it sacrifices and grain offerings that you presented to me during the forty years in the wilderness? ²⁶ But you have taken up Sakkuth your king and Kaiwan your star god, images you have made for yourselves. ²⁷ So I will send you into exile beyond Damascus." The LORD, the God of Armies, is his name. He has spoken.

Micah 6:8

Mankind, he has told each of you what is good
and what it is the LORD requires of you:
to act justly,
to love faithfulness,
and to walk humbly with your God.

Philippians 4:8-9

⁸ Finally brothers and sisters, whatever is true, whatever is honorable, whatever is just, whatever is pure, whatever is lovely, whatever is commendable—if there is any moral excellence and if there is anything praiseworthy—dwell on these things. ⁹ Do what you have learned and received and heard from me, and seen in me, and the God of peace will be with you.

Dig Deeper

Observe. What is happening in the text?

Reflect. What does it teach me about God?

Apply. What is my response?

DATE

Woe to the Complacent

Wk 2 · Day 11

AMOS 6
AMOS 7
PSALM 47
ACTS 4:13-20

Amos 6
WOE TO THE COMPLACENT

¹ Woe to those who are at ease in Zion
and to those who feel secure on the hill of Samaria—
the notable people in this first of the nations,
those the house of Israel comes to.
² Cross over to Calneh and see;
go from there to great Hamath;
then go down to Gath of the Philistines.
Are you better than these kingdoms?
Is their territory larger than yours?
³ You dismiss any thought of the evil day
and bring in a reign of violence.

⁴ They lie on beds inlaid with ivory,
sprawled out on their couches,
and dine on lambs from the flock
and calves from the stall.
⁵ They improvise songs to the sound of the harp
and invent their own musical instruments like David.
⁶ They drink wine by the bowlful
and anoint themselves with the finest oils
but do not grieve over the ruin of Joseph.
⁷ Therefore, they will now go into exile
as the first of the captives,
and the feasting of those who sprawl out
will come to an end.

ISRAEL'S PRIDE JUDGED

⁸ The Lord GOD has sworn by himself—this is the declaration of the Lord,
the God of Armies:

I loathe Jacob's pride
and hate his citadels,
so I will hand over the city and everything in it.

⁹ And if there are ten men left in one house, they will die. ¹⁰ A close
relative and burner will remove his corpse from the house. He will call to
someone in the inner recesses of the house, "Any more with you?"

That person will reply, "None."

Then he will say, "Silence, because the LORD's name must not be invoked."

¹¹ For the LORD commands:

The large house will be smashed to pieces,
and the small house to rubble.

¹² Do horses gallop on the cliffs?
Does anyone plow there with oxen?
Yet you have turned justice into poison
and the fruit of righteousness into wormwood—
¹³ you who rejoice over Lo-debar
and say, "Didn't we capture Karnaim
for ourselves by our own strength?"
¹⁴ But look, I am raising up a nation
against you, house of Israel—
 this is the declaration of the Lord,
 the GOD of Armies—
and they will oppress you
from the entrance of Hamath
to the Brook of the Arabah.

Amos 7
FIRST VISION: LOCUSTS

¹ The Lord GOD showed me this: He was forming a swarm of locusts at the time the spring crop first began to sprout—after the cutting of the king's hay. ² When the locusts finished eating the vegetation of the land, I said, "Lord GOD, please forgive! How will Jacob survive since he is so small?"

³ The LORD relented concerning this. "It will not happen," he said.

SECOND VISION: FIRE

⁴ The Lord GOD showed me this: The Lord GOD was calling for a judgment by fire. It consumed the great deep and devoured the land. ⁵ Then I said, "Lord GOD, please stop! How will Jacob survive since he is so small?"

⁶ The LORD relented concerning this. "This will not happen either," said the Lord GOD.

THIRD VISION: A PLUMB LINE

⁷ He showed me this: The Lord was standing there by a vertical wall with a plumb line in his hand. ⁸ The LORD asked me, "What do you see, Amos?"

I replied, "A plumb line."

Then the Lord said, "I am setting a plumb line among my people Israel; I will no longer spare them:

⁹ Isaac's high places will be deserted,
and Israel's sanctuaries will be in ruins;
I will rise up against the house of Jeroboam
with a sword."

AMAZIAH'S OPPOSITION

¹⁰ Amaziah the priest of Bethel sent word to King Jeroboam of Israel, saying, "Amos has conspired against you right here in the house of Israel.

The land cannot endure all his words,

¹¹ for Amos has said this: 'Jeroboam will die by the sword, and Israel will certainly go into exile from its homeland.'"

¹² Then Amaziah said to Amos, "Go away, you seer! Flee to the land of Judah. Earn your living and give your prophecies there, ¹³ but don't ever prophesy at Bethel again, for it is the king's sanctuary and a royal temple."

¹⁴ So Amos answered Amaziah, "I was not a prophet or the son of a prophet; rather, I was a herdsman, and I took care of sycamore figs. ¹⁵ But the LORD took me from following the flock and said to me, 'Go, prophesy to my people Israel.'

¹⁶ Now hear the word of the LORD. You say:

Do not prophesy against Israel;
do not preach against the house of Isaac.

¹⁷ Therefore, this is what the LORD says:

> Your wife will be a prostitute in the city,
> your sons and daughters will fall by the sword,
> and your land will be divided up
> with a measuring line.
> You yourself will die on pagan soil,
> and Israel will certainly go into exile
> from its homeland.

Psalm 47
GOD OUR KING

For the choir director. A psalm of the sons of Korah.

¹ Clap your hands, all you peoples;
shout to God with a jubilant cry.
² For the LORD, the Most High, is awe-inspiring,
a great King over the whole earth.
³ He subdues peoples under us
and nations under our feet.
⁴ He chooses for us our inheritance—
the pride of Jacob, whom he loves.   *Selah*

⁵ God ascends among shouts of joy,
the LORD, with the sound of trumpets.
⁶ Sing praise to God, sing praise;
sing praise to our King, sing praise!
⁷ Sing a song of wisdom,
for God is King of the whole earth.

⁸ God reigns over the nations;
God is seated on his holy throne.
⁹ The nobles of the peoples have assembled
with the people of the God of Abraham.
For the leaders of the earth belong to God;
he is greatly exalted.

Acts 4:13-20
THE BOLDNESS OF THE DISCIPLES

¹³ When they observed the boldness of Peter and John and realized that they were uneducated and untrained men, they were amazed and recognized that they had been with Jesus. ¹⁴ And since they saw the man who had been healed standing with them, they had nothing to say in opposition. ¹⁵ After they ordered them to leave the Sanhedrin, they conferred among themselves, ¹⁶ saying, "What should we do with these men? For an obvious sign has been done through them, clear to everyone living in Jerusalem, and we cannot deny it. ¹⁷ But so that this does not spread any further among the people, let's threaten them against speaking to anyone in this name again." ¹⁸ So they called for them and ordered them not to speak or teach at all in the name of Jesus.

¹⁹ Peter and John answered them, "Whether it's right in the sight of God for us to listen to you rather than to God, you decide; ²⁰ for we are unable to stop speaking about what we have seen and heard."

Dig Deeper

Observe. What is happening in the text?

Reflect. What does it teach me about God?

Apply. What is my response?

DATE

Judgment and Restoration

Wk 2 · Day 12

AMOS 8
AMOS 9
PSALM 53:6
EZEKIEL 37:25

Amos 8

FOURTH VISION: A BASKET OF SUMMER FRUIT

¹ The Lord God showed me this: a basket of summer fruit. ² He asked me, "What do you see, Amos?"

I replied, "A basket of summer fruit."

The Lord said to me, "The end has come for my people Israel; I will no longer spare them. ³ In that day the temple songs will become wailing"— this is the Lord God's declaration. "Many dead bodies, thrown everywhere! Silence!"

⁴ Hear this, you who trample on the needy
and do away with the poor of the land,
⁵ asking, "When will the New Moon be over
so we may sell grain,
and the Sabbath,
so we may market wheat?
We can reduce the measure
while increasing the price
and cheat with dishonest scales.
⁶ We can buy the poor with silver
and the needy for a pair of sandals
and even sell the chaff!"

⁷ The Lord has sworn by the Pride of Jacob:

I will never forget all their deeds.
⁸ Because of this, won't the land quake
and all who dwell in it mourn?
All of it will rise like the Nile;
it will surge and then subside
like the Nile in Egypt.

⁹ And in that day—
this is the declaration of the Lord God—
I will make the sun go down at noon;
I will darken the land in the daytime.
¹⁰ I will turn your feasts into mourning
and all your songs into lamentation;

I will cause everyone to wear sackcloth
and every head to be shaved.
I will make that grief
like mourning for an only son
and its outcome like a bitter day.

¹¹ Look, the days are coming—
this is the declaration of the Lord God—
when I will send a famine through the land:
not a famine of bread or a thirst for water,
but of hearing the words of the Lord.
¹² People will stagger from sea to sea
and roam from north to east
seeking the word of the Lord,
but they will not find it.
¹³ In that day the beautiful young women,
the young men also, will faint from thirst.
¹⁴ Those who swear by the guilt of Samaria
and say, "As your god lives, Dan,"
or, "As the way of Beer-sheba lives"—
they will fall, never to rise again.

Amos 9

FIFTH VISION: THE LORD BESIDE THE ALTAR

¹ I saw the Lord standing beside the altar, and he said:

Strike the capitals of the pillars
so that the thresholds shake;
knock them down on the heads of all the people.
Then I will kill the rest of them with the sword.
None of those who flee will get away;
none of the fugitives will escape.
² If they dig down to Sheol,
from there my hand will take them;
if they climb up to heaven,
from there I will bring them down.
³ If they hide
on the top of Carmel,

from there I will track them down
and seize them;
if they conceal themselves
from my sight on the sea floor,
from there I will command
the sea serpent to bite them.
⁴ And if they are driven
by their enemies into captivity,
from there I will command
the sword to kill them.
I will keep my eye on them
for harm and not for good.
⁵ The Lord, the God of Armies—
he touches the earth;
it melts, and all who dwell in it mourn;
all of it rises like the Nile
and subsides like the Nile of Egypt.
⁶ He builds his upper chambers
in the heavens
and lays the foundation of his vault
on the earth.
He summons the water of the sea
and pours it out over the surface of the earth.
The Lord is his name.

ANNOUNCEMENT OF JUDGMENT

⁷ Israelites, are you not like the Cushites to me?
    This is the Lord's declaration.
Didn't I bring Israel from the land of Egypt,
the Philistines from Caphtor,
and the Arameans from Kir?
⁸ Look, the eyes of the Lord God
are on the sinful kingdom,
and I will obliterate it
from the face of the earth.
However, I will not totally destroy
the house of Jacob—
    this is the Lord's declaration—
⁹ for I am about to give the command,
and I will shake the house of Israel
among all the nations,
as one shakes a sieve,
but not a pebble will fall to the ground.

¹⁰ All the sinners among my people
who say: "Disaster will never overtake
or confront us,"
will die by the sword.

ANNOUNCEMENT OF RESTORATION

¹¹ In that day
I will restore the fallen shelter of David:
I will repair its gaps,
restore its ruins,
and rebuild it as in the days of old,
¹² so that they may possess
the remnant of Edom
and all the nations
that bear my name—
    this is the declaration of the Lord; he will do this.

¹³ Look, the days are coming—
    this is the Lord's declaration—
when the plowman will overtake the reaper
and the one who treads grapes,
the sower of seed.
The mountains will drip with sweet wine,
and all the hills will flow with it.
¹⁴ I will restore the fortunes of my people Israel.
They will rebuild and occupy ruined cities,
plant vineyards and drink their wine,
make gardens and eat their produce.
¹⁵ I will plant them on their land,
and they will never again be uprooted
from the land I have given them.
The Lord your God has spoken.

Psalm 53:6

Oh, that Israel's deliverance would come from Zion!
When God restores the fortunes of his people,
let Jacob rejoice, let Israel be glad.

Ezekiel 37:25

They will live in the land that I gave to my servant Jacob,
where your fathers lived. They will live in it forever with their
children and grandchildren, and my servant David will be
their prince forever.

Dig Deeper

Observe. What is happening in the text?
Reflect. What does it teach me about God?
Apply. What is my response?

DATE

THE HOPE OF CHRIST'S RETURN

Give Thanks for the Book of Amos

The book of Amos is good news because it reminds us of the sovereignty of God in His involvement with His people. Amos emphasizes the coming Day of the Lord—a day which not only calls all people to account, but also boasts the hope and glory of Christ's return.

Grace Day

Wk 2 · Day 13

Take this day as an
opportunity to catch
up on your reading,
pray, and rest in the
presence of the Lord.

God reigns over the nations;
God is seated on his holy throne.

—PSALM 47:8

Weekly Truth

Memorizing Scripture is one of the best ways to carry God-breathed truth, instruction, and reproof wherever we go.

As we walk through these Minor Prophets together, we are memorizing key verses from our reading. The key verse for the book of Amos reminds us that justice and righteousness are pleasing to the Lord.

But let justice flow like water,
and righteousness, like an unfailing stream.

—AMOS 5:24

Wk 2 · Day 14

We left the artwork
on the facing page
extra light, so you
can enjoy a lesson in
hand-lettering while
meditating on the
key verse for Amos.

↓

*For this style,
we recommend
using a marker
or a felt tip pen.*

FIND THE CORRESPONDING **MEMORY CARD** PERFORATED IN THE BACK OF YOUR BOOK.

But let JUSTICE flow like water & RIGHTEOUSNESS like an unfailing Stream

03 Introduction

Saviors will ascend
Mount Zion
to rule over the hill
country of Esau,
but the kingdom will
be the LORD's.

—OBADIAH 1:21

Obadiah

SOME DISTINCTIVES:

- The name Obadiah means "servant of the LORD."

- Obadiah is the shortest book in the Old Testament.

- Obadiah takes aim at the sin of self-sufficiency (Obadiah 1:1-10).

- All we know about Obadiah is his name.

- Obadiah parallels Jeremiah 49:7-22 and Lamentations 4:22.

On the Timeline:

The time of the writing of Obadiah is disputed, with a wide variety of proposed dates from the tenth to the fifth centuries B.C., depending on when the invasion and plunder of Jerusalem occurred (vv. 11-14). The two most popular views claim that Obadiah was written during the reign of King Jehoram of Judah (around 848–841 B.C.), or shortly after the final destruction of Jerusalem by the Babylonians (586 B.C.).

A Little Background:

Obadiah was presumably the author of this book, but nothing else is known about him. His common Hebrew name is shared by at least a dozen other people in the Old Testament.

Many Prophetic Books contain prophecies against multiple nations, but the book of Obadiah focuses exclusively on the nation of Edom. Edom was the nation which descended from Esau, Jacob's twin brother and firstborn son of Isaac. Like Amos, Obadiah's short message centers on the approaching Day of the Lord, but it comes with a promise that Israel will possess the land of Edom.

Message & Purpose:

The Lord's judgment was predicted for Edom because of its arrogance in trusting geographical security (vv. 3-5), diplomatic treaties (v. 7), and the counsel of its famed wise men (v. 8; Jeremiah 49:7), instead of the true God of Israel.

Obadiah spoke of the nearness of the Day of the Lord (Isaiah 13:6; Joel 1:15; Zephaniah 1:7,14), focusing on the darkness and gloom of the Lord's wrath (Isaiah 13:6-13; Joel 2:1-3; Zephaniah 1:7-18; 2:2). Obadiah also emphasized the dual nature of the Day of the Lord. It would bring judgment on the historical nation Edom, and on "Edom" as symbolic of Israel's enemies (v. 15). At the same time, it would bring salvation for the nation of Israel (Joel 2:30-32; Zephaniah 2:1-10; 3:8-16).

Future Blessing

OBADIAH
GENESIS 27:41-42
EZEKIEL 25:12-14

Obadiah

[1] The vision of Obadiah.

EDOM'S CERTAIN JUDGMENT

This is what the Lord GOD has said about Edom:

> We have heard a message from the LORD;
> an envoy has been sent among the nations:
> "Rise up, and let us go to war against her."
> [2] Look, I will make you insignificant
> among the nations;
> you will be deeply despised.
> [3] Your arrogant heart has deceived you,
> you who live in clefts of the rock
> in your home on the heights,
> who say to yourself,
> "Who can bring me down to the ground?"
> [4] Though you seem to soar like an eagle
> and make your nest among the stars,
> even from there I will bring you down.
>   This is the LORD's declaration.
>
> [5] If thieves came to you,
> if marauders by night—
> how ravaged you would be!—
> wouldn't they steal only what they wanted?
> If grape pickers came to you,
> wouldn't they leave some grapes?
> [6] How Esau will be pillaged,
> his hidden treasures searched out!
> [7] Everyone who has a treaty with you
> will drive you to the border;
> everyone at peace with you
> will deceive and conquer you.
> Those who eat your bread
> will set a trap for you.
> He will be unaware of it.
> [8] In that day—
>   this is the LORD's declaration—
> will I not eliminate the wise ones of Edom
> and those who understand
> from the hill country of Esau?

⁹ Teman, your warriors will be terrified
so that everyone from the hill country of Esau
will be destroyed by slaughter.

EDOM'S SINS AGAINST JUDAH

¹⁰ You will be covered with shame
and destroyed forever
because of violence done to your brother Jacob.
¹¹ On the day you stood aloof,
on the day strangers captured his wealth,
while foreigners entered his city gate
and cast lots for Jerusalem,
you were just like one of them.
¹² Do not gloat over your brother
in the day of his calamity;
do not rejoice over the people of Judah
in the day of their destruction;
do not boastfully mock
in the day of distress.
¹³ Do not enter my people's city gate
in the day of their disaster.
Yes, you—do not gloat over their misery
in the day of their disaster,
and do not appropriate their possessions
in the day of their disaster.
¹⁴ Do not stand at the crossroads
to cut off their fugitives,
and do not hand over their survivors
in the day of distress.

JUDGMENT OF THE NATIONS

¹⁵ For the day of the LORD is near,
against all the nations.
As you have done, it will be done to you;
what you deserve will return on your own head.
¹⁶ As you have drunk on my holy mountain,
so all the nations will drink continually.
They will drink and gulp down
and be as though they had never been.
¹⁷ But there will be a deliverance on Mount Zion,
and it will be holy;
the house of Jacob will dispossess
those who dispossessed them.

OLD TESTAMENT PROPHETS
It was seldom a new message.

Most of the prophets did
not deliver new laws. They
usually called Israel to
obey God's existing law.

See Obadiah 1:15-18

continued

Understanding Different Kinds of Prophecy

The Minor Prophets are filled with various kinds of prophecy. Knowing the different expressions of prophecy helps us understand them and recognize where particular sections begin and end.

Here are five of the most common forms of prophetic speech:

1	2	3	4	5
The Messenger's Speech	**The Lawsuit**	**The Woe**	**The Promise**	**The Enactment**
Often beginning with "Thus says the Lord," this Is the most common form of prophecy. The prophet reminds his audience that he is only the messenger, and is therefore, one of them.	God is the plaintiff, judge, prosecutor, and bailiff in a court case against the defendant, usually a nation. The lawsuit contains, either explicitly or implicitly, a summons, a reading of charges, evidence, and a verdict.	A cry in the face of disaster, this form of prophecy includes a call of distress, the reason for the distress, and the predicted fate or doom of the person or group in distress.	Promising salvation, this kind of prophecy Is comprised of a reference to the future, a promise of coming change, and the guarantee of blessing.	The prophet not only speaks God's Word, but symbolically acts it out, or is acted upon, in some way.
AMOS 1:3-2:16 OBADIAH 1:1	ISAIAH 3:13-4:1 MICAH 6:1-16	MICAH 2:1-5 HABAKKUK 2:6-8	HOSEA 2:14-23 AMOS 9:11-15	HOSEA 1:2-5 JONAH 4:1-11

¹⁸ Then the house of Jacob will be a blazing fire,
and the house of Joseph, a burning flame,
but the house of Esau will be stubble;
Jacob will set them on fire and consume Edom.
Therefore no survivor will remain
of the house of Esau,
for the LORD has spoken.

FUTURE BLESSING FOR ISRAEL

¹⁹ People from the Negev will possess
the hill country of Esau;
those from the Judean foothills will possess
the land of the Philistines.
They will possess
the territories of Ephraim and Samaria,
while Benjamin will possess Gilead.
²⁰ The exiles of the Israelites who are in Halah
and who are among the Canaanites as far as Zarephath
as well as the exiles of Jerusalem who are in Sepharad
will possess the cities of the Negev.

²¹ Saviors will ascend Mount Zion to rule over the hill country of Esau, but the kingdom will be the LORD'S.

Genesis 27:41-42
ESAU'S ANGER

⁴¹ Esau held a grudge against Jacob because of the blessing his father had given him. And Esau determined in his heart: "The days of mourning for my father are approaching; then I will kill my brother Jacob."

⁴² When the words of her older son Esau were reported to Rebekah, she summoned her younger son Jacob and said to him, "Listen, your brother Esau is consoling himself by planning to kill you."

Ezekiel 25:12-14
JUDGMENT AGAINST EDOM

¹² This is what the Lord GOD says: Because Edom acted vengefully against the house of Judah and incurred grievous guilt by taking revenge on them, ¹³ therefore this is what the Lord GOD says: I will stretch out my hand against Edom and cut off both man and animal from it. I will make it a wasteland; they will fall by the sword from Teman to Dedan. ¹⁴ I will take my vengeance on Edom through my people Israel, and they will deal with Edom according to my anger and wrath. So they will know my vengeance. This is the declaration of the Lord GOD.

Dig Deeper

Observe. What is happening in the text?

Reflect. What does it teach me about God?

Apply. What is my response?

DATE

GOD IS ON HIS THRONE

Give Thanks for the Book of Obadiah

The book of Obadiah is good news because it displays the holiness and mercy of God. Like the book of Revelation, which proclaims the downfall of the persecuting Roman Empire, this book upholds faith in God's just government and hope in the triumph of His will. Its message reorients our aching hearts to the truth that God is on His throne, and He faithfully cares for His own.

YOU ARE A
Gracious
&
Compassionate
God

03 Introduction

Jonah

KEY VERSE

I knew that you are a gracious and compassionate God, slow to anger, abounding in faithful love, and one who relents from sending disaster.

—JONAH 4:2

SOME
DISTINCTIVES:

- The name Jonah means "dove."

- Jonah shows how God's mercy extends beyond Israel.

- Unlike most other Minor Prophets, Jonah is mostly written as a narrative, with only Jonah 2:1-9 written in poetic verse.

- Jonah emphasizes God's sovereign control over creation, the spread of His Word, and the fates of His prophets.

- Jonah contains very sophisticated writing, compared to most other Old Testament books. The book uses literary devices like metaphor, irony, humor, structure, and double meaning.

On the Timeline:

Jonah proclaimed his message to the city of Nineveh sometime in the first half of the eighth century B.C., approximately 760 B.C. His message predates the fall of the northern kingdom of Israel to Assyria in 722 B.C. Jonah also appears in 2 Kings 14:25 as a prophet from Gath-hepher (in the territory of Zebulun in northern Israel) who predicted the restoration of the northern kingdom's boundaries during the reign of Jeroboam II (c. 793–753 B.C.). This book could have been composed at any time from the eighth century to the end of the Old Testament period. The authorship of the narrative is anonymous.

A Little Background:

Jonah was called to preach to the city of Nineveh, a major Assyrian city filled with cruel people who were longtime enemies of Israel. Assyrian artwork emphasizes war, including scenes of execution, beheadings, and torture. This explains Jonah's reluctance to preach to this infamous city of warlike people.

Message & Purpose:

Jonah's message emphasizes God's compassion for and pursuit of the Gentiles. In chapter 1, Gentile sailors learn to revere and worship Israel's God. And in chapter 3, Nineveh's repentance shows that Gentiles, too, can be saved. God's "merciful and compassionate" (4:2) actions toward Nineveh show that the God of the Old Testament is a God of grace.

The book of Jonah also portrays the sovereign power of God over the natural world. God can create a storm (1:4), miraculously raise up a plant as well as a worm to kill it (4:6-7), and use a great fish to swallow and save a wayward prophet like Jonah (1:17).

The book of Jonah expresses the futility of running from God. The trouble Jonah got into when he tried to escape God's calling is a warning to readers that running from God is futile and only invites unnecessary hardship.

Jonah's Call

Wk 3 · Day 16

OLD TESTAMENT PROPHETS
They were appointed by God.

Prophets did not appoint themselves. The Lord pronounced harsh judgment on false prophets because they assumed authority but did not speak God's Word.

See Jonah 1:1-2

Jonah 1
JONAH'S FLIGHT

¹ The word of the LORD came to Jonah son of Amittai:

² "Get up! Go to the great city of Nineveh

and preach against it because their evil has come up before me." ³ Jonah got up to flee to Tarshish from the LORD's presence. He went down to Joppa and found a ship going to Tarshish. He paid the fare and went down into it to go with them to Tarshish from the LORD's presence.

⁴ But the LORD threw a great wind onto the sea, and such a great storm arose on the sea that the ship threatened to break apart. ⁵ The sailors were afraid, and each cried out to his god. They threw the ship's cargo into the sea to lighten the load. Meanwhile, Jonah had gone down to the lowest part of the vessel and had stretched out and fallen into a deep sleep.

⁶ The captain approached him and said, "What are you doing sound asleep? Get up! Call to your god. Maybe this god will consider us, and we won't perish."

⁷ "Come on!" the sailors said to each other. "Let's cast lots. Then we'll know who is to blame for this trouble we're in." So they cast lots, and the lot singled out Jonah. ⁸ Then they said to him, "Tell us who is to blame for this trouble we're in. What is your business, and where are you from? What is your country, and what people are you from?"

⁹ He answered them, "I'm a Hebrew. I worship the LORD, the God of the heavens, who made the sea and the dry land."

¹⁰ Then the men were seized by a great fear and said to him, "What is this you've done?" The men knew he was fleeing from the Lord's presence because he had told them. ¹¹ So they said to him, "What should we do to you so that the sea will calm down for us?" For the sea was getting worse and worse.

¹² He answered them, "Pick me up and throw me into the sea so that it will calm down for you, for I know that I'm to blame for this great storm that is against you." ¹³ Nevertheless, the men rowed hard to get back to

dry land, but they couldn't because the sea was raging against them more and more.

14 So they called out to the LORD: "Please, LORD, don't let us perish because of this man's life, and don't charge us with innocent blood! For you, LORD, have done just as you pleased." 15 Then they picked up Jonah and threw him into the sea, and the sea stopped its raging. 16 The men were seized by great fear of the LORD, and they offered a sacrifice to the LORD and made vows.

17 The LORD appointed a great fish to swallow Jonah, and Jonah was in the belly of the fish three days and three nights.

Psalm 104:24-26

24 How countless are your works, LORD!
In wisdom you have made them all;
the earth is full of your creatures.
25 Here is the sea, vast and wide,
teeming with creatures beyond number—
living things both large and small.
26 There the ships move about,
and Leviathan, which you formed to play there.

Matthew 12:38-42

THE SIGN OF JONAH

38 Then some of the scribes and Pharisees said to him, "Teacher, we want to see a sign from you."

39 He answered them, "An evil and adulterous generation demands a sign, but no sign will be given to it except the sign of the prophet Jonah. 40 For as Jonah was in the belly of the huge fish three days and three nights, so the Son of Man will be in the heart of the earth three days and three nights. 41 The men of Nineveh will stand up at the judgment with this generation and condemn it, because they repented at Jonah's preaching; and look—something greater than Jonah is here. 42 The queen of the south will rise up at the judgment with this generation and condemn it, because she came from the ends of the earth to hear the wisdom of Solomon; and look—something greater than Solomon is here."

Dig Deeper

Observe. What is happening in the text?

Reflect. What does it teach me about God?

Apply. What is my response?

DATE

Jonah's Prayer

Wk 3 · Day 17

JONAH 2
PSALM 88:4-5
HEBREWS 4:16

Jonah 2

JONAH'S PRAYER

¹ Jonah prayed to the Lord his God from the belly of the fish:

² I called to the Lord in my distress,
and he answered me.
I cried out for help from deep inside Sheol;
you heard my voice.
³ You threw me into the depths,
into the heart of the seas,
and the current overcame me.
All your breakers and your billows swept over me.
⁴ But I said, "I have been banished
from your sight,
yet I will look once more
toward your holy temple.
⁵ The water engulfed me up to the neck;
the watery depths overcame me;
seaweed was wrapped around my head.
⁶ I sank to the foundations of the mountains,
the earth's gates shut behind me forever!

Then you raised my life from the Pit, Lord my God!

⁷ As my life was fading away,
I remembered the Lord,
and my prayer came to you,
to your holy temple.
⁸ Those who cherish worthless idols
abandon their faithful love,
⁹ but as for me, I will sacrifice to you
with a voice of thanksgiving.
I will fulfill what I have vowed.
Salvation belongs to the Lord."

¹⁰ Then the Lord commanded the fish, and it vomited Jonah onto dry land.

Psalm 88:4-5

⁴ I am counted among those going down to the Pit.
I am like a man without strength,
⁵ abandoned among the dead.
I am like the slain lying in the grave,
whom you no longer remember,
and who are cut off from your care.

Hebrews 4:16

Therefore, let us approach the throne of grace with boldness, so that we may receive mercy and find grace to help us in time of need.

 the CALL   TARSHISH   the STORM   NINEVEH

Dig Deeper

Observe. What is happening in the text?

Reflect. What does it teach me about God?

Apply. What is my response?

DATE

Jonah's Preaching

Wk 3 · Day 18

JONAH 3
JEREMIAH 18:7-10
NAHUM 1:2-11

Jonah 3
JONAH'S PREACHING

[1] The word of the LORD came to Jonah a second time: [2] "Get up! Go to the great city of Nineveh and preach the message that I tell you." [3] Jonah got up and went to Nineveh according to the LORD's command.

Now Nineveh was an extremely great city, a three-day walk. [4] Jonah set out on the first day of his walk in the city and proclaimed, "In forty days Nineveh will be demolished!"

[5] Then the people of Nineveh believed God.

They proclaimed a fast and dressed in sackcloth—from the greatest of them to the least.

[6] When word reached the king of Nineveh, he got up from his throne, took off his royal robe, put on sackcloth, and sat in ashes. [7] Then he issued a decree in Nineveh:

By order of the king and his nobles: No person or animal, herd or flock, is to taste anything at all. They must not eat or drink water. [8] Furthermore, both people and animals must be covered with sackcloth, and everyone must call out earnestly to God. Each must turn from his evil ways and from his wrongdoing. [9] Who knows? God may turn and relent; he may turn from his burning anger so that we will not perish.

[10] God saw their actions—that they had turned from their evil ways—so God relented from the disaster he had threatened them with. And he did not do it.

Jeremiah 18:7-10

[7] At one moment I might announce concerning a nation or a kingdom that I will uproot, tear down, and destroy it. [8] However, if that nation about which I have made the announcement turns from its evil, I will relent concerning the disaster I had planned to do to it. [9] At another time I might announce concerning a nation or a kingdom that I will build and plant it. [10] However, if it does what is evil in my sight by not listening to me, I will relent concerning the good I had said I would do to it.

Nahum 1:2-11
GOD'S VENGEANCE

² The Lord is a jealous and avenging God;
the Lord takes vengeance
and is fierce in wrath.
The Lord takes vengeance against his foes;
he is furious with his enemies.
³ The Lord is slow to anger but great in power;
the Lord will never leave the guilty unpunished.
His path is in the whirlwind and storm,
and clouds are the dust beneath his feet.
⁴ He rebukes the sea and dries it up,
and he makes all the rivers run dry.
Bashan and Carmel wither;
even the flower of Lebanon withers.
⁵ The mountains quake before him,
and the hills melt;
the earth trembles at his presence—
the world and all who live in it.
⁶ Who can withstand his indignation?
Who can endure his burning anger?
His wrath is poured out like fire;
even rocks are shattered before him.

DESTRUCTION OF NINEVEH

⁷ The Lord is good,
a stronghold in a day of distress;
he cares for those who take refuge in him.
⁸ But he will completely destroy Nineveh
with an overwhelming flood,
and he will chase his enemies into darkness.

⁹ Whatever you plot against the Lord,
he will bring it to complete destruction;
oppression will not rise up a second time.
¹⁰ For they will be consumed
like entangled thorns,
like the drink of a drunkard
and like straw that is fully dry.
¹¹ One has gone out from you,
who plots evil against the Lord,
and is a wicked counselor.

Dig Deeper

Observe. What is happening in the text?

Reflect. What does it teach me about God?

Apply. What is my response?

DATE

Jonah's Anger

Jonah 4
JONAH'S ANGER

¹ Jonah was greatly displeased and became furious. ² He prayed to the Lord:

"Please, Lord, isn't this what I thought while I was still in my own country? That's why I fled toward Tarshish in the first place. I knew that you are a gracious and compassionate God, slow to anger, abounding in faithful love, and one who relents from sending disaster.

³ And now, Lord, take my life from me, for it is better for me to die than to live."

⁴ The Lord asked, "Is it right for you to be angry?"

⁵ Jonah left the city and found a place east of it. He made himself a shelter there and sat in its shade to see what would happen to the city. ⁶ Then the Lord God appointed a plant, and it grew over Jonah to provide shade for his head to rescue him from his trouble. Jonah was greatly pleased with the plant. ⁷ When dawn came the next day, God appointed a worm that attacked the plant, and it withered.

[8] As the sun was rising, God appointed a scorching east wind. The sun beat down on Jonah's head so much that he almost fainted, and he wanted to die. He said, "It's better for me to die than to live."

[9] Then God asked Jonah, "Is it right for you to be angry about the plant?"

"Yes, it's right!" he replied. "I'm angry enough to die!"

[10] So the LORD said, "You cared about the plant, which you did not labor over and did not grow. It appeared in a night and perished in a night. [11] But may I not care about the great city of Nineveh, which has more than a hundred and twenty thousand people who cannot distinguish between their right and their left, as well as many animals?"

Acts 11:15-18

[15] "As I began to speak, the Holy Spirit came down on them, just as on us at the beginning. [16] I remembered the word of the Lord, how he said, 'John baptized with water, but you will be baptized with the Holy Spirit.' [17] If, then, God gave them the same gift that he also gave to us when we believed in the Lord Jesus Christ, how could I possibly hinder God?"

[18] When they heard this they became silent. And they glorified God, saying, "So then, God has given repentance resulting in life even to the Gentiles."

Romans 5:6-11
THOSE DECLARED RIGHTEOUS ARE RECONCILED

[6] For while we were still helpless, at the right time, Christ died for the ungodly. [7] For rarely will someone die for a just person—though for a good person perhaps someone might even dare to die. [8] But God proves his own love for us in that while we were still sinners, Christ died for us. [9] How much more then, since we have now been declared righteous by his blood, will we be saved through him from wrath. [10] For if, while we were enemies, we were reconciled to God through the death of his Son, then how much more, having been reconciled, will we be saved by his life. [11] And not only that, but we also rejoice in God through our Lord Jesus Christ, through whom we have now received this reconciliation.

Dig Deeper

Observe. What is happening in the text?

Reflect. What does it teach me about God?

Apply. What is my response?

DATE

SALVATION OFFERED TO THE WHOLE WORLD

Give Thanks for the Book of Jonah

The book of Jonah is good news because it shows that God's gift of salvation is offered to the whole world—not just Israel. It displays God's power over nature, and the futility of ignoring His instruction. Jonah's time in the fish foreshadows Jesus' burial and resurrection, pointing to Christ's ultimate fulfillment of the salvation Jonah himself preached.

Grace Day

Wk 3 · Day 20

Take this day as an
opportunity to catch
up on your reading,
pray, and rest in the
presence of the Lord.

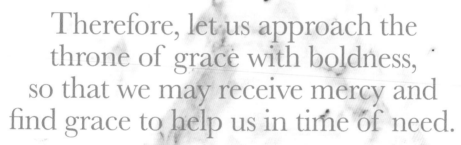

Therefore, let us approach the
throne of grace with boldness,
so that we may receive mercy and
find grace to help us in time of need.

—HEBREWS 4:16

Weekly Truth

Memorizing Scripture is one of the best ways to carry God-breathed truth, instruction, and reproof wherever we go.

As we walk through these Minor Prophets together, we are memorizing key verses from our reading. The key verse for the book of Jonah reminds us of God's compassion.

I knew that you are a gracious and compassionate God, slow to anger, abounding in faithful love, and one who relents from sending disaster.

—JONAH 4:2

We left the artwork on the facing page extra light, so you can enjoy a lesson in hand-lettering while meditating on the key verse for Jonah.

↓

For this style of lettering, we suggest using a felt tip pen or pencil.

Wk 3 · Day 21

YOU ARE
A
Gracious
&
Compassionate
God

Act Justly,
Love Faithfulness,
Walk Humbly
with
Your God

04 Introduction

Micah

KEY VERSE

Mankind, he has told each of you what is good and what it is the LORD requires of you: to act justly, to love faithfulness, and to walk humbly with your God.

—MICAH 6:8

SOME DISTINCTIVES:

- The name Micah means "no one is like Yahweh."

- Micah's call to be a prophet was never recorded, and he was never named as a prophet, but his message was "filled with power by the Spirit of the LORD" (Micah 3:8).

- Micah shows us that the Lord who scatters His people in judgment is also the Shepherd-King who will gather them (2:12-13; 4:6-8).

- Micah is an example of a "lawsuit" prophecy.

- Micah teaches that God's saving grace in the past assures us of His saving grace in the present and future (7:14-20).

On the Timeline:

Micah's ministry likely began late in Jotham's reign and ended early in Hezekiah's, dating between 730 and 690 B.C. His reference to the future judgment of Samaria (1:6) shows that his ministry began some time before Israel's destruction in 722 B.C., indicating that Micah's ministry overlapped Isaiah's.

A Little Background:

Micah's hometown of Moresheth-gath (1:1,14) in the lowlands of Judah was about 25 miles southwest of Jerusalem. The mentioning of his hometown suggests that Micah probably ministered elsewhere, including Jerusalem. Since no genealogy is given, we can presume he did not come from a prominent family. Micah was a skilled orator, a master of metaphors with a genius for wordplay and blunt, vivid imagery. Few prophets saw the future more

clearly. Micah prophesied the fall of Samaria (1:5-9), Jerusalem's destruction (1:1-16; 3:12), the Babylonian captivity and return from exile (4:6-10), as well as the birth of Christ in Bethlehem (5:2).

Message & Purpose:

Micah sought "to proclaim to Jacob his rebellion and to Israel his sin" (3:8), pronouncing God's judgment in an effort to call His people to repentance. Injustice was rampant in Israel at the time (2:1-2; 3:1-3; 6:10-11), and the people would suffer destruction and exile (1:10-16), silence from God (3:6-7), and frustration (6:13-16). But Micah balanced his prophecy with hope of a remnant spared through God's judgment, and a glorious future restoration (2:12-13; 4:1-5; 5:5-9; 7:8-20).

Micah's Lament

Wk 4 · Day 22

MICAH 1
MICAH 2
PSALM 46
HEBREWS 6:13-20

Micah 1

¹ The word of the LORD that came to Micah the Moreshite—what he saw regarding Samaria and Jerusalem in the days of Jotham, Ahaz, and Hezekiah, kings of Judah.

COMING JUDGMENT ON ISRAEL

² Listen, all you peoples;
pay attention, earth and everyone in it!
The Lord GOD will be a witness against you,
the Lord, from his holy temple.
³ Look, the LORD is leaving his place
and coming down to trample
the heights of the earth.
⁴ The mountains will melt beneath him,
and the valleys will split apart,
like wax near a fire,
like water cascading down a mountainside.
⁵ All this will happen because of Jacob's rebellion
and the sins of the house of Israel.
What is the rebellion of Jacob?
Isn't it Samaria?
And what is the high place of Judah?
Isn't it Jerusalem?
⁶ Therefore, I will make Samaria
a heap of ruins in the countryside,
a planting area for a vineyard.
I will roll her stones into the valley
and expose her foundations.
⁷ All her carved images will be smashed to pieces;
all her wages will be burned in the fire,
and I will destroy all her idols.
Since she collected the wages of a prostitute,
they will be used again for a prostitute.

MICAH'S LAMENT

⁸ Because of this I will lament and wail;
I will walk barefoot and naked.
I will howl like the jackals
and mourn like ostriches.
⁹ For her wound is incurable
and has reached even Judah;
it has approached my people's city gate,
as far as Jerusalem.

¹⁰ Don't announce it in Gath,

don't weep at all.

Roll in the dust in Beth-leaphrah.

¹¹ Depart in shameful nakedness,

you residents of Shaphir;

the residents of Zaanan will not come out.

Beth-ezel is lamenting;

its support is taken from you.

¹² Though the residents of Maroth

anxiously wait for something good,

disaster has come from the Lord

to the gate of Jerusalem.

¹³ Harness the horses to the chariot,

you residents of Lachish.

This was the beginning of sin for Daughter Zion

because Israel's acts of rebellion can be traced to you.

¹⁴ Therefore, send farewell gifts to Moresheth-gath;

the houses of Achzib are a deception

to the kings of Israel.

¹⁵ I will again bring a conqueror

against you who live in Mareshah.

The nobility of Israel will come to Adullam.

¹⁶ Shave yourselves bald and cut off your hair

in sorrow for your precious children;

make yourselves as bald as an eagle,

for they have been taken from you into exile.

Micah 2
OPPRESSORS JUDGED

¹ Woe to those who dream up wickedness and prepare evil plans on their beds!

At morning light they accomplish it

because the power is in their hands.

² They covet fields and seize them;

they also take houses.

They deprive a man of his home,

a person of his inheritance.

³ Therefore, the Lord says:

I am now planning a disaster

against this nation;

you cannot free your necks from it.

Then you will not walk so proudly

because it will be an evil time.

⁴ In that day one will take up a taunt against you

and lament mournfully, saying,

"We are totally ruined!

He measures out the allotted land of my people.

How he removes it from me!

He allots our fields to traitors."

⁵ Therefore, there will be no one

in the assembly of the Lord

to divide the land by casting lots.

GOD'S WORD REJECTED

⁶ "Quit your preaching," they preach.
"They should not preach these things;
shame will not overtake us."
⁷ House of Jacob, should it be asked,
"Is the Spirit of the LORD impatient?
Are these the things he does?"
Don't my words bring good
to the one who walks uprightly?
⁸ But recently my people have risen up
like an enemy:

You strip off the splendid robe
from those who are passing through confidently,
like those returning from war.
⁹ You force the women of my people
out of their comfortable homes,
and you take my blessing
from their children forever.
¹⁰ Get up and leave,
for this is not your place of rest

because defilement brings
destruction—
a grievous destruction!
¹¹ If a man comes
and utters empty lies—
"I will preach to you about wine
and beer"—
he would be just the preacher for
this people!

¹² I will indeed gather all of you, Jacob;
I will collect the remnant of Israel.
I will bring them together like sheep in a pen,
like a flock in the middle of its pasture.
It will be noisy with people.
¹³ One who breaks open the way
will advance before them;
they will break out, pass through the city gate,
and leave by it.
Their King will pass through before them,
the LORD as their leader.

Psalm 46
GOD OUR REFUGE

For the choir director. A song of the sons of Korah.
According to Alamoth.

¹ God is our refuge and strength,
a helper who is always found
in times of trouble.
² Therefore we will not be afraid,
though the earth trembles
and the mountains topple
into the depths of the seas,
³ though its water roars and foams
and the mountains quake with its turmoil.   *Selah*

⁴ There is a river—
its streams delight the city of God,
the holy dwelling place of the Most High.
⁵ God is within her; she will not be toppled.
God will help her when the morning dawns.
⁶ Nations rage, kingdoms topple;
the earth melts when he lifts his voice.
⁷ The LORD of Armies is with us;
the God of Jacob is our stronghold.   *Selah*

⁸ Come, see the works of the LORD,
who brings devastation on the earth.

⁹ He makes wars cease throughout the earth.
He shatters bows and cuts spears to pieces;
he sets wagons ablaze.
¹⁰ "Stop your fighting, and know that I am God,
exalted among the nations, exalted on the earth."
¹¹ The LORD of Armies is with us;
the God of Jacob is our stronghold.   *Selah*

Hebrews 6:13-20
INHERITING THE PROMISE

¹³ For when God made a promise to Abraham, since he had no one greater to swear by, he swore by himself: ¹⁴ I will indeed bless you, and I will greatly multiply you. ¹⁵ And so, after waiting patiently, Abraham obtained the promise. ¹⁶ For people swear by something greater than themselves, and for them a confirming oath ends every dispute. ¹⁷ Because God wanted to show his unchangeable purpose even more clearly to the heirs of the promise, he guaranteed it with an oath, ¹⁸ so that through two unchangeable things, in which it is impossible for God to lie, we who have fled for refuge might have strong encouragement to seize the hope set before us. ¹⁹ We have this hope as an anchor for the soul, firm and secure. It enters the inner sanctuary behind the curtain. ²⁰ Jesus has entered there on our behalf as a forerunner, because he has become a high priest forever according to the order of Melchizedek.

Dig Deeper

Observe. What is happening in the text?
Reflect. What does it teach me about God?
Apply. What is my response?

DATE

From Exile to Victory

Wk 4 · Day 23

MICAH 3
MICAH 4
PSALM 25:8-9
I CORINTHIANS 10:31

OLD TESTAMENT PROPHETS
They had authority.

Prophets held their office in
the same way priests and
kings did. They were given
the authority to speak God's
truth to people in power
without fear of retribution.

See Micah 3:1

Micah 3

UNJUST LEADERS JUDGED

[1] Then I said, "Now listen, leaders of Jacob,
you rulers of the house of Israel.
Aren't you supposed to know what is just?
[2] You hate good and love evil.
You tear off people's skin
and strip their flesh from their bones.
[3] You eat the flesh of my people
after you strip their skin from them
and break their bones.
You chop them up
like flesh for the cooking pot,
like meat in a cauldron."
[4] Then they will cry out to the LORD,
but he will not answer them.
He will hide his face from them at that time
because of the crimes they have committed.

FALSE PROPHETS JUDGED

[5] This is what the LORD says
concerning the prophets
who lead my people astray,
who proclaim peace
when they have food to sink their teeth into
but declare war against the one
who puts nothing in their mouths.
[6] Therefore, it will be night for you—
without visions;
it will grow dark for you—
without divination.
The sun will set on these prophets,
and the daylight will turn black over them.
[7] Then the seers will be ashamed
and the diviners disappointed.
They will all cover their mouths
because there will be no answer from God.

[8] As for me, however, I am filled with power
by the Spirit of the LORD,
with justice and courage,
to proclaim to Jacob his rebellion
and to Israel his sin.

ZION'S DESTRUCTION

9 Listen to this, leaders of the house of Jacob,
you rulers of the house of Israel,
who abhor justice
and pervert everything that is right,
10 who build Zion with bloodshed
and Jerusalem with injustice.
11 Her leaders issue rulings for a bribe,
her priests teach for payment,
and her prophets practice divination for silver.
Yet they lean on the Lord, saying,
"Isn't the LORD among us?
No disaster will overtake us."
12 Therefore, because of you,
Zion will be plowed like a field,
Jerusalem will become ruins,
and the temple's mountain
will be a high thicket.

Micah 4
THE LORD'S RULE FROM RESTORED ZION

1 In the last days
the mountain of the LORD's house
will be established
at the top of the mountains
and will be raised above the hills.
Peoples will stream to it,
2 and many nations will come and say,
"Come, let us go up to the mountain of the LORD,
to the house of the God of Jacob.
He will teach us about his ways
so we may walk in his paths."
For instruction will go out of Zion
and the word of the LORD from Jerusalem.
3 He will settle disputes among many peoples
and provide arbitration for strong nations
that are far away.
They will beat their swords into plows
and their spears into pruning knives.
Nation will not take up the sword against nation,
and they will never again train for war.

4 But each person will sit under his grapevine
and under his fig tree
with no one to frighten him.
For the mouth of the LORD of Armies
has spoken.
5 Though all the peoples each walk
in the name of their gods,
we will walk in the name of the LORD
our God
forever and ever.

6 On that day—
this is the LORD's declaration—
I will assemble the lame
and gather the scattered,
those I have injured.
7 I will make the lame into a remnant,
those far removed into a strong nation.
Then the LORD will reign over them in
Mount Zion
from this time on and forever.
8 And you, watchtower for the flock,
fortified hill of Daughter Zion,
the former rule will come to you;
sovereignty will come to Daughter
Jerusalem.

FROM EXILE TO VICTORY

9 Now, why are you shouting loudly?
Is there no king with you?
Has your counselor perished
so that anguish grips you like a woman
in labor?
10 Writhe and cry out, Daughter Zion,
like a woman in labor,
for now you will leave the city
and camp in the open fields.
You will go to Babylon;
there you will be rescued;

there the LORD will redeem you
from the grasp of your enemies!
11 Many nations have now assembled
against you;
they say, "Let her be defiled,
and let us feast our eyes on Zion."
12 But they do not know the Lord's intentions
or understand his plan,
that he has gathered them
like sheaves to the threshing floor.
13 Rise and thresh, Daughter Zion,
for I will make your horns iron
and your hooves bronze
so you can crush many peoples.
Then you will set apart their plunder
for the LORD,
their wealth for the Lord of the whole earth.

Psalm 25:8-9

8 The LORD is good and upright;
therefore he shows sinners the way.
9 He leads the humble in what is right
and teaches them his way.

1 Corinthians 10:31

So, whether
you eat or
drink, or what-
ever you do,
do everything
for the glory
of God.

Dig Deeper

Observe. What is happening in the text?

Reflect. What does it teach me about God?

Apply. What is my response?

DATE

From Defeated Ruler to Conquering King

Wk 4 · Day 24

MICAH 5
PSALM 72:1-11
LUKE 1:26-33

Micah 5
FROM DEFEATED RULER TO CONQUERING KING

[1] Now, daughter who is under attack,
you slash yourself in grief;
a siege is set against us!
They are striking the judge of Israel
on the cheek with a rod.
[2] Bethlehem Ephrathah,
you are small among the clans of Judah;
one will come from you
to be ruler over Israel for me.
His origin is from antiquity,
from ancient times.
[3] Therefore, Israel will be abandoned until the time
when she who is in labor has given birth;
then the rest of the ruler's brothers will return
to the people of Israel.
[4] He will stand and shepherd them
in the strength of the LORD,
in the majestic name of the LORD his God.
They will live securely,
for then his greatness will extend
to the ends of the earth.

[5] He will be their peace.

When Assyria invades our land,
when it marches against our fortresses,
we will raise against it seven shepherds,
even eight leaders of men.
[6] They will shepherd the land of Assyria with the sword,
the land of Nimrod with a drawn blade.
So he will rescue us from Assyria
when it invades our land,
when it marches against our territory.

THE GLORIOUS AND PURIFIED REMNANT

[7] Then the remnant of Jacob
will be among many peoples
like dew from the LORD,

like showers on the grass,
which do not wait for anyone
or linger for mankind.
⁸ Then the remnant of Jacob
will be among the nations, among many peoples,
like a lion among animals of the forest,
like a young lion among flocks of sheep,
which tramples and tears as it passes through,
and there is no one to rescue them.
⁹ Your hand will be lifted up against your adversaries,
and all your enemies will be destroyed.

¹⁰ In that day—
    this is the Lord's declaration—
I will remove your horses from you
and wreck your chariots.
¹¹ I will remove the cities of your land
and tear down all your fortresses.
¹² I will remove sorceries from your hands,
and you will not have any more fortune-tellers.
¹³ I will remove your carved images
and sacred pillars from you
so that you will no longer worship
the work of your hands.
¹⁴ I will pull up the Asherah poles from among you
and demolish your cities.
¹⁵ I will take vengeance in anger and wrath
against the nations that have not obeyed me.

Psalm 72:1-11
A PRAYER FOR THE KING

Of Solomon.

¹ God, give your justice to the king
and your righteousness to the king's son.
² He will judge your people with righteousness
and your afflicted ones with justice.
³ May the mountains bring well-being to the people
and the hills, righteousness.
⁴ May he vindicate the afflicted among the people,
help the poor,
and crush the oppressor.

⁵ May they fear you while the sun endures
and as long as the moon, throughout all generations.
⁶ May the king be like rain that falls on the cut grass,
like spring showers that water the earth.
⁷ May the righteous flourish in his days
and well-being abound
until the moon is no more.

⁸ May he rule from sea to sea
and from the Euphrates
to the ends of the earth.
⁹ May desert tribes kneel before him
and his enemies lick the dust.
¹⁰ May the kings of Tarshish
and the coasts and islands bring tribute,
the kings of Sheba and Seba offer gifts.
¹¹ Let all kings bow in homage to him,
all nations serve him.

Luke 1:26-33
GABRIEL PREDICTS JESUS' BIRTH

²⁶ In the sixth month, the angel Gabriel was sent by God to a town in Galilee called Nazareth, ²⁷ to a virgin engaged to a man named Joseph, of the house of David. The virgin's name was Mary. ²⁸ And the angel came to her and said, "Greetings, favored woman! The Lord is with you." ²⁹ But she was deeply troubled by this statement, wondering what kind of greeting this could be. ³⁰ Then the angel told her: "Do not be afraid, Mary, for you have found favor with God. ³¹ Now listen: You will conceive and give birth to a son, and you will name him Jesus. ³² He will be great and will be called the Son of the Most High, and the Lord God will give him the throne of his father David. ³³ He will reign over the house of Jacob forever, and his kingdom will have no end."

Dig Deeper

Observe. What is happening in the text?
Reflect. What does it teach me about God?
Apply. What is my response?

DATE

God's Lawsuit Against Judah

Wk 4 · Day 25

MICAH 6
JEREMIAH 22:3
COLOSSIANS 3:12-17

OLD TESTAMENT PROPHECY
It was all relational.

Although the prophetic books often deal with concepts like famine, displacement, and God's judgment, the fact that they exist shows God is in an ongoing relationship with His audience.

See Micah 6:3-5

Micah 6
GOD'S LAWSUIT AGAINST JUDAH

¹ Now listen to what the LORD is saying:

Rise, plead your case before the mountains,
and let the hills hear your complaint.
² Listen to the LORD's lawsuit,
you mountains and enduring foundations of the earth,
because the LORD has a case against his people,
and he will argue it against Israel.
³ My people, what have I done to you,
or how have I wearied you?
Testify against me!
⁴ Indeed, I brought you up from the land of Egypt
and redeemed you from that place of slavery.
I sent Moses, Aaron, and Miriam ahead of you.
⁵ My people,
remember what King Balak of Moab proposed,
what Balaam son of Beor answered him,
and what happened from the Acacia Grove to Gilgal
so that you may acknowledge
the LORD's righteous acts.

⁶ What should I bring before the LORD
when I come to bow before God on high?
Should I come before him with burnt offerings,
with year-old calves?
⁷ Would the LORD be pleased with thousands of rams
or with ten thousand streams of oil?
Should I give my firstborn for my transgression,
the offspring of my body for my own sin?

⁸ Mankind, he has told each of you what is good
and what it is the LORD requires of you:

to act justly, to love faithfulness, and to walk humbly with your God.

VERDICT OF JUDGMENT

⁹ The voice of the LORD calls out to the city
(and it is wise to fear your name):
"Pay attention to the rod
and the one who ordained it.
¹⁰ Are there still the treasures of wickedness
and the accursed short measure
in the house of the wicked?
¹¹ Can I excuse wicked scales
or bags of deceptive weights?
¹² For the wealthy of the city are full of violence,
and its residents speak lies;
the tongues in their mouths are deceitful.

¹³ "As a result, I have begun to strike you severely,
bringing desolation because of your sins.
¹⁴ You will eat but not be satisfied,
for there will be hunger within you.
What you acquire, you cannot save,
and what you do save,
I will give to the sword.
¹⁵ You will sow but not reap;
you will press olives
but not anoint yourself with oil;
and you will tread grapes
but not drink the wine.
¹⁶ The statutes of Omri
and all the practices of Ahab's house
have been observed;
you have followed their policies.
Therefore, I will make you a desolate place
and the city's residents an object of contempt;
you will bear the scorn of my people."

Jeremiah 22:3

This is what the LORD says: Administer justice and righteousness. Rescue the victim of robbery from his oppressor. Don't exploit or brutalize the resident alien, the fatherless, or the widow. Don't shed innocent blood in this place.

Colossians 3:12-17
THE CHRISTIAN LIFE

¹² Therefore, as God's chosen ones, holy and dearly loved, put on compassion, kindness, humility, gentleness, and patience, ¹³ bearing with one another and forgiving one another if anyone has a grievance against another. Just as the Lord has forgiven you, so you are also to forgive. ¹⁴ Above all, put on love, which is the perfect bond of unity. ¹⁵ And let the peace of Christ, to which you were also called in one body, rule your hearts. And be thankful. ¹⁶ Let the word of Christ dwell richly among you, in all wisdom teaching and admonishing one another through psalms, hymns, and spiritual songs, singing to God with gratitude in your hearts. ¹⁷ And whatever you do, in word or in deed, do everything in the name of the Lord Jesus, giving thanks to God the Father through him.

Dig Deeper

Observe. What is happening in the text?

Reflect. What does it teach me about God?

Apply. What is my response?

DATE

Micah's Prayer Answered

Wk 4 · Day 26

MICAH 7
PSALM 103:8-9
ROMANS 6:12-14

Micah 7

ISRAEL'S MORAL DECLINE

1 How sad for me!
For I am like one who—
when the summer fruit has been gathered
after the gleaning of the grape harvest—
finds no grape cluster to eat,
no early fig, which I crave.
2 Faithful people have vanished from the land;
there is no one upright among the people.
All of them wait in ambush to shed blood;
they hunt each other with a net.
3 Both hands are good at accomplishing evil:
the official and the judge demand a bribe;
when the powerful man communicates his evil desire,
they plot it together.
4 The best of them is like a brier;
the most upright is worse than a hedge of thorns.
The day of your watchmen,
the day of your punishment, is coming;
at this time their panic is here.
5 Do not rely on a friend;
don't trust in a close companion.
Seal your mouth
from the woman who lies in your arms.
6 Surely a son considers his father a fool,
a daughter opposes her mother,
and a daughter-in-law is against her mother-in-law;
a man's enemies are the men of his own household.
7 But I will look to the LORD;
I will wait for the God of my salvation.
My God will hear me.

ZION'S VINDICATION

8 Do not rejoice over me, my enemy!
Though I have fallen, I will stand up;
though I sit in darkness,
the LORD will be my light.
9 Because I have sinned against him,
I must endure the LORD's rage
until he champions my cause

and establishes justice for me.
He will bring me into the light;
I will see his salvation.
¹⁰ Then my enemy will see,
and she will be covered with shame,
the one who said to me,
"Where is the Lᴏʀᴅ your God?"
My eyes will look at her in triumph;
at that time she will be trampled
like mud in the streets.

¹¹ A day will come for rebuilding your walls;
on that day your boundary will be extended.
¹² On that day people will come to you
from Assyria and the cities of Egypt,
even from Egypt to the Euphrates River
and from sea to sea
and mountain to mountain.
¹³ Then the earth will become a wasteland
because of its inhabitants
and as a result of their actions.

MICAH'S PRAYER ANSWERED

¹⁴ Shepherd your people with your staff,
the flock that is your possession.
They live alone in a woodland
surrounded by pastures.
Let them graze in Bashan and Gilead
as in ancient times.

¹⁵ I will perform miracles for them
as in the days of your exodus
from the land of Egypt.
¹⁶ Nations will see and be ashamed
of all their power.
They will put their hands over their mouths,
and their ears will become deaf.
¹⁷ They will lick the dust like a snake;
they will come trembling out of their hiding places
like reptiles slithering on the ground.
They will tremble in the presence of the Lᴏʀᴅ our God;
they will stand in awe of you.

¹⁸ Who is a God like you,
forgiving iniquity and passing over rebellion
for the remnant of his inheritance?

He does not hold on to his anger forever because he delights in faithful love.

¹⁹ He will again have compassion on us;
he will vanquish our iniquities.
You will cast all our sins
into the depths of the sea.
²⁰ You will show loyalty to Jacob
and faithful love to Abraham,
as you swore to our fathers
from days long ago.

Psalm 103:8-9

⁸ The Lᴏʀᴅ is compassionate and gracious,
slow to anger and abounding in faithful love.
⁹ He will not always accuse us
or be angry forever.

Romans 6:12-14

¹² Therefore do not let sin reign in your mortal body, so that you obey its desires. ¹³ And do not offer any parts of it to sin as weapons for unrighteousness. But as those who are alive from the dead, offer yourselves to God, and all the parts of yourselves to God as weapons for righteousness. ¹⁴ For sin will not rule over you, because you are not under the law but under grace.

Dig Deeper

Observe. What is happening in the text?

Reflect. What does it teach me about God?

Apply. What is my response?

DATE

A HEART TUNED TO GOD

Give Thanks for the Book of Micah

The book of Micah is good news because it demonstrates that God is holy and just, and He demands holiness and justice from all people. Micah's audience had grown content to go through religious motions without genuine devotion. But Micah preached that true religion comes from a heart tuned to God, resulting in godly living. Those who refuse to repent will face God's judgment, but the faithful will find His salvation and be led by God's king, who would usher in His peace and prosperity.

Grace Day

Wk 4 · Day 27

Take this day as an
opportunity to catch
up on your reading,
pray, and rest in the
presence of the Lord.

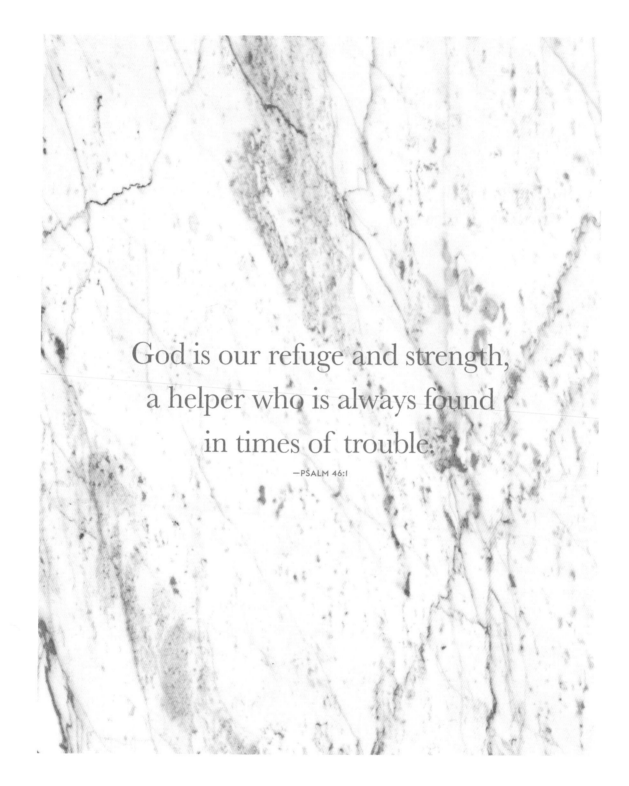

God is our refuge and strength,
a helper who is always found
in times of trouble.

—PSALM 46:1

Weekly Truth

Memorizing Scripture is one of the best ways to carry God-breathed truth, instruction, and reproof wherever we go.

As we walk through these Minor Prophets together, we are memorizing key verses from our reading. The key verse for the book of Micah tells us how God calls His people to live.

Mankind, he has told each of you what is good
and what it is the LORD requires of you:
to act justly,
to love faithfulness,
and to walk humbly with your God.

—MICAH 6:8

We left the artwork
on the facing page
extra light, so you
can enjoy a lesson in
hand-lettering while
meditating on the key
verse for Micah.

↓

*We like using
a brush pen or
a paint brush
to achieve this
style of lettering.*

Wk 4 · Day 28

Act Justly,
Love Faithfulness,
Walk Humbly
with
your God

Where did I study?

- O HOME
- O CHURCH
- O OFFICE
- O A FRIEND'S HOUSE
- O COFFEE SHOP
- O OTHER

DID I LISTEN TO MUSIC?

ARTIST:

SONG:

SCRIPTURE I WILL
SHARE WITH A FRIEND:

WHEN DID I HAVE MY BEST STUDYING SUCCESS?

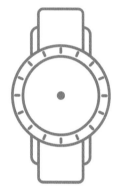

WHAT WAS HAPPENING IN THE WORLD?

What was my best takeaway?

WHAT WAS MY BIGGEST FEAR?

What was my greatest comfort?

_____

_____

_____

_____

_____

_____

I LEARNED THESE UNEXPECTED NEW THINGS:

1

2

3

END DATE

| MONTH | DAY | YEAR |

COLOPHON

This book was printed offset in Nashville, Tennessee, on 70# Lynx Opaque. Typefaces used include Baskerville, Garamond, and Euclid.
Cover is printed offset on Tango 12 pt C1S with a soft-touch matte laminate. Finished size is 8"x10".

EDITORS-IN-CHIEF:
Raechel Myers and Amanda Bible Williams

CONTENT DIRECTOR:
Russ Ramsey, MDiv., ThM.

EDITORS:
Rebecca Faires and Kara Gause

EDITORIAL ASSISTANT:
Ellen Taylor

ADDITIONAL THEOLOGICAL OVERSIGHT:
Nate Shurden, MDiv.

CREATIVE DIRECTOR:
Ryan Myers

ART DIRECTOR:
Amanda Barnhart

DESIGNER & MAP ARTIST:
Kelsea Allen

LETTERERS:
Patrick Laurent (14), Chris Vinca (44), Dan Lee (82),
Cymone Wilder (92), Carrie Shyrock (116)

COVER & INTERIOR PHOTOGRAPHERS:
Jordan and Landon Thompson

SUBSCRIPTION INQUIRIES:
orders@shereadstruth.com

She Reads Truth is a worldwide community of women who read God's Word together every day.

Founded in 2012, She Reads Truth invites women of all ages to engage with Scripture through daily reading plans, online conversation led by a vibrant community of contributors, and offline resources created at the intersection of beauty, goodness, and Truth.

STOP BY

shereadstruth.com

SHOP

shopshereadstruth.com

KEEP IN TOUCH

@shereadstruth

DOWNLOAD THE APP

SEND A NOTE

hello@shereadstruth.com

CONNECT

#SheReadsTruth

Oh, the fullness,
pleasure, sheer
excitement of knowing
God on Earth!

— JIM ELLIOT